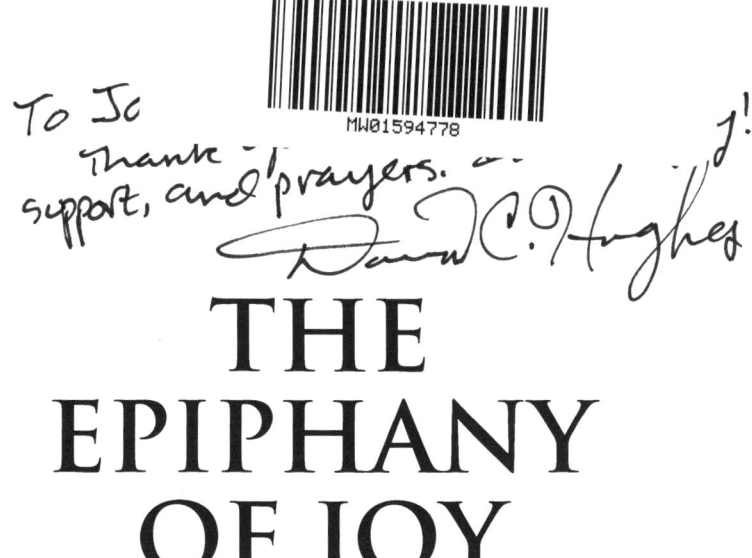

To Jo
Thanks...
support, and prayers. ...
...j!
David C. Hughes

THE
EPIPHANY
OF JOY

DAVID C. HUGHES

RISING PHOENIX PRESS

Copyright © 2014 by David C. Hughes.
Visit http://davidchugheswriter.com.

Published by Progressive Rising Phoenix Press.
Visit www.progressiverisingphoenix.com.

Printed in the U.S.A.

ISBN-10: 1940834163
ISBN-13: 978-1-940834-16-0

1st Printing

Edited by Robyn Conley.
Visit http://robynconley.com/.

Cover photo credit: Bigstock Photo
http://www.bigstockphoto.com

Original butterfly illustrations copyright © 2014.
All rights reserved by Emilie L. Hughes.

Author photographs taken by Dennis Post of Platinum Shots, copyright © 2014.
All rights reserved by Dennis Post.
Visit www.platinumshots.com.

Book Layout and Cover Design by William Speir.
Visit www.williamspeir.com.

SCRIPTURAL
REFERENCES

DEDICATION

To God – here You go, assignment complete. Thank You for all those little kisses on the cheek; You make me laugh! I hope I make You laugh, too.

To Mary, my most amazing wife – your faith in God, in me, and in this process has done more than you'll ever know to help me stay the course. You are truly a Proverbs 31 wife.

And to Hannah, my precious and beautiful daughter – you, my darling, are the epitome of pure joy. Thank you for modeling joy, God's love, and what it means to trust unconditionally.

I love you more than mere words can express!

ACKNOWLEDGEMENTS

Mom and Dad – without your love I wouldn't be here, and without your guidance and discipline I wouldn't be the man I am today. My family and the world will reap the benefits of your dedication, grit, and true love.

My sister, Linda Hughes Dewhirst – thank you for listening to your guardian angel, and thank you for sharing your butterfly dreams. Look! They landed on the covers! Keep smiling, keep learning, and keep dreaming, my dear sis.

Emilie Hughes – you're an awesome niece, you know that? And so amazingly talented. Thanks for illustrating both *Melted Clowns* and for creating the original butterfly artwork for *The Epiphany of Joy*. You are a blessing and I look forward to working with you for years to come.

Amanda Thrasher and Jannifer Powelson, co-founders of Progressive Rising Phoenix Press – I appreciate with all my heart the trust and confidence you have in me and in my capabilities, and I look forward to this great adventure you've helped make possible. You ladies rock!

Robyn Conley, book doctor, fellow writer, friend – wow, it's been a long road, hasn't it? Thanks for your excellent editing, your words of encouragement, and for helping me to get through those dark times so long ago. You are truly a friend.

Marc Owings, founder of elevateHim Ministries – you are anointed, bro! Thank you for being obedient to the call the Lord has placed in your heart to encourage and build up His Kingdom. Without your obedience this work may never have been written.

Jeff Catt, my former manager – thank you for listening to your crazy employee's testimony and for supporting me along the way. Your faith has helped open the door to answering Jesus' call to spread the Good News to all nations. Thank you for believing!

Dennis Post, photographer, crazy Dutch guy, friend – your ability to bend light and capture essence is truly amazing! Thank you for living out your passion – the joy in what you love to do brought out the joy in what I love to do.

All the folks who shared your stories with me – you have changed my life and I'm eternally grateful for your courage, enthusiasm, and patience during this process. Nothing's more powerful than your testimonies, and by allowing me to convey them in this book, they will become even more powerful.

My blog followers – thank you for keeping me motivated to continue turning the crank, and thank you all for your support, prayers, and interest as we travel on this incredible journey together. Without you my life's calling would be meaningless. With you the world is truly blessed.

And my fellow writers, especially the members of the Fort Worth Writers – thank you for helping me realize I'm not alone in this craziness.

TABLE OF CONTENTS

INTRODUCTION

"Do not grieve, for the joy of the LORD is your strength."
— Nehemiah 8:10

I shall be telling this with a sigh
Somewhere ages and ages hence:
Two roads diverged in a wood, and I –
I took the one less traveled by,
And that has made all the difference.
— Robert Frost, "The Road Not Taken"[1]

In January 2011, during a Christian men's retreat in Lake Fork, Texas, God wrote me a letter. And the scales fell off my eyes...

In June 2011, while on a business trip to Buffalo, New York, God spoke to me. And my world changed...

A week later, while sparring with the devil in the shower, God whispered to me. And things solidified...

I was raised a child of the 60's and 70's, immersed in a middle-class, hard-working, country-boy environment. My dad, the first of his immediate family to transition out of a blue-collar upbringing into the white-collar world of Big Blue, worked for IBM in Endicott, New York. I grew up in the rural town of Maine, New York, with two younger brothers and a baby sister in a 1,200-square-foot ranch-style house. The joke was our town contained more cows than people, and the smell, especially on stagnant mid-summer afternoons, testified to the verity of that claim.

My parents instilled in my siblings and me a strong family experience, a Catholic-based spiritual foundation, and a solid work ethic. They demonstrated the lessons daily as we did life together in that cozy three-bedroom avocado green house with one bathroom. Thanks to Dad, I gained an appreciation for storytelling, walks in the woods, and being an involved parent. And thanks to my first-generation Italian-American mom, I gained an appreciation for polka music, meticulousness, and talking with my hands! Both my parents came from humble and challenging backgrounds, and they used that experience to teach us love, family, and integrity. They made (and, after more than 51 years of marriage, still make) a great team.

When I was in elementary school, Mom showed me how to run the old Kirby upright with the olive-green bag. When I turned twelve or thirteen, Dad demonstrated the ins and outs of starting and using the simple but dependable Craftsman push mower to cut our half-acre, hilly lawn. To this day I remember having to yank the cable off the spark plug to stop that beast. I quickly learned what 15,000 volts feels like, and what it does to your hand muscles. I took on babysitting jobs at age thirteen and started working for a family-owned department store and an ice cream shop at sixteen. I maintained flowerbeds and lawns for the church and for neighbors, and I even helped a local dairy farmer harvest hay. I learned the value of hard work, responsibility, and making and saving money. There was no question I was going to continue my education straight out of high school into college, earn a degree, and procure a good-paying job.

The joy of childhood filled my heart in those days. My siblings and I spent hours playing in the basement and romping in the fields and forests surrounding our house. I built plastic model airplanes, flew balsa wood radio-controlled aircraft, and graduated to piloting full-scale sail-planes over the pasture-embossed hills of New York's Southern Tier region. With a knack for all things mechanical, I spent endless hours re-building lawnmowers found in junk heaps, play-ing with small engines, and riding motorcycles in the woods. I tore down, cleaned up, and rebuilt a Honda CR125 dirt bike on the front porch with no manual and no previous experience with two-stroke engines – I just rolled up my sleeves and dug in. The engine started right up after I put it all back together without a single leftover part!

We spent cold winter days building forts in snow drifts, and frigid winter nights sledding in the darkness down quarter-mile bobsled runs

Dad built for us and the neighborhood kids. I reveled in my creativity while in junior and senior high school, enjoying drawing, writing, collecting butterflies, and producing a couple of hilarious Super 8 movies. And even as my dream of becoming an Air Force pilot crashed due to a stomach ulcer I'd developed in my junior year, I still chased my creative outlets post-high school as I pursued a bachelor's degree in electrical engineering.

But somewhere between my sophomore and junior years of college, boredom, upheaval, unreasonable fear, and discontent roared in, body-slamming joy to the mat while I worked my first co-op job in the structured and demanding environment of a tech company. Another bleeding ulcer almost killed me. A surgeon removed my duodenum and the lower third of my stomach, and I caught a brief glimpse of the power and enticement of Demerol. I read Stephen King's *The Talisman* while in the hospital and questioned deeply the path I struggled down. At that moment I stood in Robert Frost's yellow wood, at the divergence of the two roads, and I made a choice: I took the one leading to the completion of my degree and the start of a career in the military aircraft industry which lasted almost three decades.

Double-mindedness about my vocation versus my avocation, a failed marriage, a slump into clinical depression, a hyperactive sensitivity to the size of my bank accounts, and a six-year loss of my voice came close to pinching out the flame of joy between fingers of despair and hopelessness. Whatever joy I had left retreated to the dark corners of my memory, wide-eyed, shivering, waiting. It darted out to celebrate my engagement and marriage to my second (and final) wife, Mary, the birth of our daughter, Hannah, and the first flight of the jet fighter I helped build. Joy's voice emerged occasionally to sing high harmony to the songs I made up for Hannah, and it listened with rapt attention to the stories we created and laughed about. But somewhere along the way I'd all but left joy on the side of the road to die.

Thankfully, it didn't.

In January 2011 I attended a Fully Alive men's weekend with Marc Owings, Pastor of elevateHim Ministries in Fort Worth, and co-author of *The Original Sanctuary* and *The ALL IN Life*. At one point during the weekend the facilitators provided the men with an opportunity for focused one-on-one time with God, and during that time God spoke to me through a letter penned by my own hand, directed by the Spirit. "Set your heart right," God wrote to me. "Set your eyes on Me, and KNOW, *KNOW*, in your heart of hearts that you are going down the right path, that you are fulfilling My plans, and the plans are to give you joy, *fun*, and to prosper you in ways you can't even imagine. You'll know when it's time to transition; trust that I am right now creating these paths and opportunities for you. You'll know. And write to your (and My) heart's content! Enjoy and be filled with joy! This is the path." The scales fell off my eyes as I realized I'd been on the right road – the Road to

Damascus – all along. I cried a lot that weekend. We all did.

Fast-forward six months. While on a business trip to Buffalo, New York, to engage with one of my suppliers, the Lord whispered to me in the hotel room: "I want you to write a book about joy," He said. "I want you to become a joy expert." *Me? Write a book about joy?* I sounded an awful lot like Moses at that instant. Until then my writing had focused more on short horror stories, newspaper articles, a novel reminiscent of a *Twilight Zone* marathon, and poetry rather than Christian non-fiction. Who was I to talk about joy, let alone write a book about it? What did I know?

Turns out, I didn't have to know anything; I just had to be obedient to God's request. But a week after that trip to Buffalo, Satan attacked my mind with a full-on frontal assault: "You'll never finish the book," he tormented. "Who are you to write about joy?" I stood in the shower, water splashing over me, praying to God and rebuking the devil.

"Lord," I pleaded. "How am I going to write this thing?"

"All you have to do is be creative and organize it," He replied. *Ha! That's all?* But I knew He was right; creativity and organization are two gifts the Lord had planted in my being from the start, so it really was that simple.

Scott Crenshaw, Senior Pastor of New River Fellowship in Hudson Oaks, Texas, once said, "There is something when the winds of persecution blow on the flames of God in your heart."

Satan's rancid breath tried to blow out my joy completely. But instead, he inadvertently helped fan the flames into an inferno of hope. As usual, God upended the devil and his plans, turning his evil intentions into the good of God's Kingdom. Yay, Jesus! Through researching and writing this book, I've discovered how God means for us to live, not in slavery to expectations but in the freedom of who He created us to be. God opened my eyes and heart to what it means to lead a joy-filled life overflowing with the Spirit, despite circumstances and past choices.

As I started writing *The Epiphany of Joy*, I was far from being a joy expert, and I concurred with my friend Stephen Erwin when he told me, "Joy is a decision – it doesn't come naturally to me." It doesn't come naturally to me either, although by the smile on my face, my persistence, and my sense of humor you'd never guess that. That's the funny thing about joy: it shows even when it's not felt.

This joy thing continues to be a journey from despair and depression and hopelessness to trust and hope and praise. I know this will be a lifelong adventure, a continuous education, and a reminder that joy is a gift planted in me by the Spirit of God. I need to remember to unwrap that gift and receive it daily in my heart. Like the tattoo on my arm declaring my sonship with the King of kings and Lord of lords, it's there, I just gotta show it!

So... what is joy? I mean, what is it *really*? Is it equivalent to happiness? Why is it so elusive in today's world? Why do so many people rely on

Things and Feelings and Money and People for
joy, and never really experience it at all? Joy is in
my daughter's squeal of delight as she runs
across the back yard and launches herself into
her inflatable swimming pool. It's climbing up to
cloud base in a sailplane on nothing but the
breath of heated air. It's continuing to plant my
butt in my chair in front of the computer every
day because I can be confident the Lord has put
me in this and all my past jobs to train me for a
mission way bigger than myself. It's shouldering
my cross and pressing through the depression,
knowing Jesus' power is made perfect in my
weakness. It's the birth of a baby, the first
moment of contact between her and me, despite
the fear.

Despite. This is a key word. Joy is *despite*.
Joy is in the trials. Joy is in the calmness. Joy is
in the seeing what others can't see, doing what
others think is strange, maybe even foolish,
living a life focused on obedience to God rather
than centering around myself. "Do not conform to
the pattern of this world," the Apostle Paul wrote
in his epistle to the church in Rome, "but be
transformed by the renewing of your mind"
(Romans 12:2). This command is prefaced in the
verse prior, with the offer of our bodies – ourselves – to God, wholly and completely, without
reservation.

Joy is a renewing, an attitude provided by
grace by the Spirit who moves in us, by a God
who loves us more than we'll ever know or could
even fathom. As Bob Hamp, former Freedom
Pastor at Gateway Church in Southlake, Texas,

told me: "Joy is a way of looking at the world. It may not be okay now, but it will be." So step out in faith with me and let's learn about this thing called "joy" together. We don't have to worry about taking the wrong path – it's not the ending that counts, but the way we get there.

Enjoy!

CHAPTER 1
THE SEARCH FOR JOY

All of us are coming to Joy. Life, in confronting us with our fears, will see to that. The more vigorously we take on life and gather experiences, the more quickly we learn the lesson.
— Todd Evan Pressman, Ph.D.,
Radical Joy[2]

No riches are greater than a healthy body; and no happiness than a joyful heart.
— Ben Sira 30:16 (NABRE)

When I first set out to write this book, I had no definite idea what joy was. I mean, I sorta kinda had an inkling, like what I experienced the first time I rode a thermal up to cloud base in a Schweizer 1-26 sailplane and scratched the misty gray belly of a cumulous swollen with rain. The intense thrill, the pounding heart, the shout of thanks to God – in that moment a window flew open and joy blew in on a favorable wind. It was a little taste, a little crumb, that, once experienced, remained on the tongue of my soul ever since. Like C.S. Lewis described in *Surprised by Joy*, the experience of joy "is that of an unsatisfied desire which is itself more desirable than any other satisfaction."[3]

Or when I'd walk into a bookstore and inhale the comforting smell of books, the scent of ink and glue and paper and hope, the aroma of dreams realized and purpose secured. The same feeling that rose in my heart when that fat gray cloud enveloped my sailplane would again erupt from deep in my gut and choke me up. The feeling was so heady, so enticing I'd tell people I could drop my engineering job and work in a bookstore just to be close to the books and the people who read them. Another nugget, another crumb.

Or the moment my baby entered the world, when my wife, Mary, lay under the blue sheets, her round belly painted amber with Betadine, her scared eyes searching mine as the doctor made the incision to pull out our stubbornly-breeched child. "You can look now," the obstetrician called to me as the moment arrived. I stood up and peered over the cloth barrier just as the doctor grabbed hold of our baby's ankles and tugged. Before I knew it he cradled that long, chubby, surprisingly clean infant in gloved hands. "Okay, Dad, tell everyone what it is."

I was overwhelmed. Mary and I had made the decision months earlier to wait until the baby was born to find out its sex. Somewhere along the way the nurse midwives began using "he" and "his" during our weekly checkups, so we were convinced they'd let the baby out of the bassinet. We just knew it was a "he." So as Mary's tear-filled blue eyes grew wider over my wordlessness, and as I looked down at this purple and pink life covered with a bit of cheesy yellow vernix, I had no idea what the swollen thing was between its plump legs. It didn't *look* like a boy's parts. "You do know what it is, don't you?" the doctor implored. And in that moment of emotional overload, joy slid in and coaxed my voice into action as I realized God had playfully answered my prayers.

"It's a... girl!" I cried. I turned to Mary. "It's Hannah!" Thus God delivered Hannah Elizabeth Hughes into the world, a little brown-eyed mirror reflecting my looks and Mary's attitude, a reminder of God's grace, love, and sense of humor, joy wrapped in an eight pound three ounce package of pure dependence.

But as I mentioned earlier, joy does not come naturally to me, so I have to be willing to accept it supernaturally. I experience its fullness in little nuggets: a shooting star on a morning walk, my wife's touch, my daughter's jokes. I have a tendency to wallow around in the muck of woe, to drag through the quicksand of depression, to slump through the mire of sadness, to loll in bouts of low energy. I'm as inflexible as a stick, and I don't respond well to changes in plans. Instead of savoring each moment God gives me, I analyze my present reality against a backdrop of the past and the what-ifs of the future. I have a hard time living God's commands in Isaiah 43:18-19:

> *Forget the former things;*
> *do not dwell on the past.*
> *See, I am doing a new thing!*
> *Now it springs up; do you not perceive it?*

or Jesus' imperative delivered during the Sermon on the Mount:

> *Therefore do not worry about tomorrow, for tomorrow will worry about itself. Each day has enough trouble of its own.*
> — Matthew 6:34

I can slip in and out of self-pity as quickly as my daughter can slip in and out of her entire wardrobe of dress-up clothes. But maybe my ignorance of joy's reality has skewed my experience of it. Maybe it's a matter of perspective. Maybe, just maybe, I do live joyfully; I just don't fully realize it.

I'd heard the word "joy" all my life, but when it came right down to it, I couldn't tell you exactly what it was, couldn't describe it concisely, couldn't wrap it up into a comprehensible analogy. I know what depression is. I know what sadness is. I know what frustration is. I know what boredom is. But I didn't know what joy is. Is joy different from happiness? Is it an emotion? A feeling? A state of being? Is joy something to strive for, or is it something innate? Or does it fully manifest only after being born again? Can everyone experience joy, or only those with a well-developed spiritual foundation? Or no foundation at all? Can only children experience and demonstrate consistent joy, the way my memories of childhood testify to, or can adults loaded down with baggage and histories and conformity and material desires and "stuff" experience it, too?

Possessing strong perfectionistic tendencies, and being educated as an engineer, I look at the world in black-and-white rather than in blends of RGB. As such, I can overlook the obvious, overcomplicate the simple, and overthink things. Sometimes it's hard for me to get out of my own way. Mary doesn't call me "Hard Way" for nothing. Even though I'm not as literal as Jim Parsons' character, Sheldon Cooper, in "The Big Bang Theory," I can be smart-but-dense nonetheless.

So, like a good writer (and good scientist), I investigated the dictionary definition of joy, but came away dissatisfied: is joy really a fuller, more vibrant shade of happiness? Or is it something totally different? I realized I didn't even know how to define happiness, let alone joy. Ugh! I'm a man of many words, but when God ordained this book, He stumped me.

Which was precisely His point.

Kathryn Hannah Marie is a cheerful 62-year-old massage therapist and ordained minister, as petite and exuberant as her little pink house. One evening Mary, Hannah, and I met several of Mary's friends, including Kathryn, for dinner at a Mexican restaurant in Fort Worth's vibrant 7th Street district. I sat across from Kathryn, who wears her age as gracefully as her smile, and we chatted while waiting for our orders to arrive. Suddenly Hannah slipped out of the chair between Mary and me, ran around the end of the table, and hopped into Kathryn's lap. Kathryn wrapped her arms around her, pulled her close, and began to sing in a beautiful bird-like voice that reminded me of Snow White. "What's joy?" I asked as Hannah relaxed and her rambunctious energy settled into quiet contentment.

"Joy is an attitude," Kathryn replied, a common answer I'd received from other folks living squarely in the palm of Joy's hand. "I choose to be joyful."

A couple months later, after a massage, I asked Kathryn the same question. "We can choose," she reiterated. "The same situation can present itself to two different people and those two different people are going to handle it differently because of their choices. If I choose to get angry over something I have no control over, suddenly it has control over me." She confessed she does, on occasion, get angry, but she recognizes the anger, wrestles it down, and moves on. "Instead of letting it destroy my whole day or my whole week or whatever, I just get past it," she declared. "Resolving issues keeps you from dwelling on them. I really think that what we do with our situations determines whether we express joy or not."

"You know more about joy than you think you do," my friend, Bill Kelly, affirmed one evening after I'd talked to him about God's joy-filled assignment. "You exude it." But as I mentioned, I tend to overlook the obvious: if joy was a snake, I would've been bitten by it a long time ago. Hmm. Death by joy... Not a bad prospect, is it?

I have to acknowledge that, as Bill pointed out, I do come across as being a joy-filled guy. People used to call me "Smiley" because I wear a smile as comfortably as a pair of old sandals. I smile at everyone, and if I see you approaching, I'll shoot you a friendly "Good morning," or "How are you?" Yes, I am that weirdo. Most of the time I receive a smile back, or a "Fine, how are you?" Rarely do I get the blank stare, the averted eyes, or a frown.

"You have a very joyous countenance," Kathryn Marie confirmed, her kind eyes twinkling as she spoke. "I think you live joy. I see it in your face, you know: the wrinkles that you have and the wrinkles that I have are the same – they're smiling!"

The problem is in thinking of joy as an emotion; after all, that's what we've generally been taught. That's what the dictionary says – joy is defined as intense or great happiness. That's what the secular world declares it. But it's not the whole picture. Far from it. The struggle I've had with defining joy, driving to the heart of joy, comes down to one simple fact: the world's definition is different from God's definition. The world's idea of happiness is based on things, on attachments, on fleeting moments, on circumstances, on addictions. Joy transcends all of that.

One Holy Saturday morning, Mary and I attended a briefing with other church nursery workers on the procedures for checking in, tending to, and checking out the dozens of children expected to arrive for the next morning's Easter services. Before the orientation started, Catherine Talbot, a fellow New River member and a woman who lives joyfully despite circumstances, hustled past us and took a seat. You gotta love her: she glows with joy and doesn't even know it! Mary and I jumped up, ran over to where she sat, and hugged her. "You're one of the people I want to interview for my joy book," I told her.

"Me?" she gasped. "Do you really see it?"

"Lady," Mary said, "You wear it!"

I then asked her what she thought joy was. "It's a knowing," she said. "Knowing God is in control." Not an emotion, a *knowing*. Another piece of the puzzle clicked into place.

"Joy is a place where I exist," described Heath Jackson, owner of Jackson Creative and an ordained Apple Store Genius. "Whether you choose to live there or not." Not an emotion, a place. Click!

His wife, Mary, agreed. "Happiness is a response to circumstance, and joy is there despite circumstance. We were created for God's pleasure which brings Him joy, so it's rooted in pleasing God, in God's pleasure."

Heath nodded. "Joy is a place where God has called us to be when we're walking in His presence. I call it the cycle of joy: His greatest pleasure is seeing us getting His glory, and our greatest pleasure is when we're in His presence obeying Him and hearing Him and walking in His grace. Jesus did nothing except through the Father. That's the only reason we humans don't walk as close to God as Jesus did. Joy is knowing you're walking in His will." Not an emotion... a knowing. Like Catherine Talbot said.

During my interview with Kathryn Marie, she suggested I go right to the source and interview Hannah, who was five at the time. After all, Jesus Himself declared, "Unless you change and become like little children, you will never enter the kingdom of heaven" (Matthew 18:3). So one day, after finishing lunch, I looked right into her big brown eyes and asked, "What's joy?"

She hesitated, then answered quietly: "I don't know. Nice, happy?" *Sounds like my answer*, I thought.

"Why don't you ask your guardian angel?" I suggested.

"Okay," she beamed. She held up her blue plastic Fisher Price telephone. "I'll ask Faith. She knows a lot about joy." She proceeded to punch the plastic buttons on the fake plastic phone. "Do you know what her number is, Daddy?" I shook my head. "It's 1-5-4-2." She then put the phone to her ear and walked into the living room. "Hello? Faith?" She chit-chatted with her angel for a moment, then asked her, "What's joy?" Silence. "Happiness. Okay, thanks." She hung up and walked back into the dining room where I still sat, watching. "Joy is happiness, Dad," she said.

Joy is happiness, yet so much more. Joy was watching my daughter make that call to her guardian angel using a toy phone. Joy was the smile on her face when she delivered the angel's response. Joy was confirming Hannah still has one foot planted firmly on heaven's threshold. Joy is a state of mind, a state of being, a continuity with God; when we are in God's presence, we are unshakably joy-filled. Joy is a fruit of the Spirit, as the Apostle Paul wrote in his epistle to the Galatians (see Galatians 5:22). And "since we live by the Spirit, let us keep in step with the Spirit" (Galatians 5:25).

Joy is a choice. Joy is a knowing. Joy is a place. Joy is a command. To the church in Philippi, the Apostle Paul, while in prison, wrote, "Rejoice in the Lord always. I will say it again: Rejoice!" (Philippians 4:4). To the church in Thessalonica, he exhorted, "Rejoice always, pray continually, give thanks in all circumstances; for this is God's will for you in Christ Jesus" (1 Thessalonians 5:16-18). And to the Christian church in Rome, he charged, "Be joyful in hope, patient in affliction, faithful in prayer" (Romans 12:12).

Rejoicing and being joyful is God's will! Joy is not passive; it is fulfilled in the expression. Joy, though a noun, is brought to life, is made active, by expressing it. In other words, rejoice! It's so much more fulfilling – and fun – than grumbling, complaining, and wallowing around in the black clay of selfishness and bad attitude. As believers, Jesus called us to be a light for the world. What better way is there to shine that light than to live every moment, every opportunity, and every sacrifice immersed in joy?

One day I had to run to Target to return a pair of flip-flops Hannah couldn't wear. After I parked, I hopped out and opened Hannah's door. As is our habit, she automatically reached up and grabbed my hand after I'd shut the door and locked the car. "Dad," she said as we walked across the parking lot. "Holding your hand is joy." I can't think of a better definition of joy than that, can you?

CHAPTER 2
JOY IN GOD'S WORD

In the beginning was the Word, and the Word was with God, and the Word was God.
– John 1:1

Productive thinking disrupts unproductive thinking. You overcome evil with good. And when you preoccupy your mind with God's Word, you go a long way toward shutting out temptation.
– Tommy Newberry, The 4:8 Principle: The Secret to a Joy-Filled Life[4]

If you haven't already guessed it, Hannah's a great kid. Yes, I'm a teensy bit biased, but she really is awesome. She's got a great memory, unshakable persistence, and a command of the English language just like her dad. She's got a spunky attitude, confidence, and a natural wisdom just like her mom. And she sings better than either of us (especially Mary). She's strong, she's persistent, she's got a giving heart, and she's an amazing prayer warrior. All around, she's **sigh** perfect... Well, there is one character trait that drives both Mary and I to the wine fridge on occasion, and if you have children you'll agree it's a chronic symptom of childhood. What am I talking about? Disobedience. Yep, good old-fashioned not listening when told to do something. Thank you, Adam and Eve.

"Why are you so *mean* to me?" Hannah gripes when we get onto her case for disobeying.

"Because you don't do what you're told!" we reply, teeth gritted, voices one notch above annoyance and a hair below outright anger. "If you'd only listen to us, we'd never have to spank your butt or yell at you or put you in time out!"

I can just imagine God smiling and nodding His head knowingly, a twinkle in His all-seeing eye. Yep, pot calling the kettle black and all that. As the Apostle Paul wrote in his letter to the Romans, "for all have sinned and fall short of the glory of God" (Romans 3:23). Disobedience is at the heart of our sinful nature. How often do you attend church and listen to the sermon, or dial the radio to hear the message, or click on a Spirit-guided blog and read the Word without giving it a second thought? Don't raise your hands all at once.

James wrote in his letter to the twelve tribes in dispersion, "Do not merely listen to the word, and so deceive yourselves. Do what it says" (James 1:22). Those of us who have reached the golden age of reason can be just as obstinate about obeying God's edicts as a child is about obeying her parents' commands. No wonder joy seems elusive sometimes; we shoo it away ourselves!

Throughout the Old Testament, God constantly reminded the Jewish people of the benefits of obeying His precepts, and the consequences of disobeying them. Leviticus 26:1-13 clearly spells out these benefits in plain Hebrew: "'If you follow my decrees and are careful to obey my commands, I will send you rain in its season, and the ground will yield its crops and the trees their fruit'" (Leviticus 26:3-4). In verses 5 through 13, God promised abundant food to eat, strength to defeat their enemies, and to hang out with them.

In verses 14 through 39, God just as clearly spells out the consequences of disobedience: "'But if you will not listen to me and carry out all these commands, and if you reject my decrees and abhor my laws and fail to carry out all my commands and so violate my covenant, then I will do this to you: I will bring on you sudden terror, wasting diseases and fever that will destroy your sight and sap your strength. You will plant seed in vain, because your enemies will eat it'" (Leviticus 26:14-16). Like the Lorrie Morgan lyric says, "What part of no don't you understand?" When the Hebrews didn't listen, they got sent to timeout – a lot. And they got spanked a bunch, too.

In the New Testament, Jesus told His disciples before going to the cross, "If you keep my commands, you will remain in my love, just as I have kept my Father's commands and remain in his love. I have told you this so that my joy may be in you and that your joy may be complete. My command is this: Love each other as I have loved you" (John 15:10-12). Yes, Jesus fulfilled the Old Testament Law, but He still expects us to obey the commands He gave us out of love, for our own good, and the good of all His people. As parents, Mary and I seem to constantly tell Hannah, "All you have to do is obey and you won't get into trouble." Likewise, listening to God's Word, believing it, and obeying it will keep trouble at arm's length, with the subsequent benefit of remaining in joy. All we gotta do is love! And listen!

In my experience growing up, my only exposure to Scripture was during mass, when the lector read the weekly first and second readings, and when the priest read the Gospel then preached on it during his homily. I was well-versed in my Catechism, I could recite prayers by heart, and I regularly received the Sacraments, but I don't remember reading much Scripture. As a consequence I entered adulthood without a strong appreciation for God's Word and its power and capacity to instill joy.

In his second letter to Timothy, the Apostle Paul encouraged Timothy to not only remember Scripture, but to use it as a tool for becoming wise and for doing good. "But as for you," Paul wrote, "continue in what you have learned and have become convinced of, because you know those from whom you learned it, and how from infancy you have known the Holy Scriptures, which are able to make you wise for salvation through faith in Christ Jesus. All Scripture is God-breathed and is useful for teaching, rebuking, correcting and training in righteousness, so that the servant of God may be thoroughly equipped for every good work" (2 Timothy 3:14-17).

My first exposure to the power of God's Word and its ability to bring about healing and change manifested when I read Norman Vincent Peale's book, *The Power of Positive Thinking.* When I discovered this little book and the message it conveyed, I was struggling with the first wave of unsettledness conjured by the tug of writing versus the practicality of engineering. From the time I could remember I'd always been a worrier, and this book ushered in a new way of looking at circumstances, dreams, and desires. My desire to write stood in stark contrast to the desire to live financially secure, and my inability to reconcile the conflict dragged me physically, mentally, and spiritually into the dark basement of depression and dissatisfaction. But *The Power of Positive Thinking* turned on a light in the form of Philippians 4:13 (KJV): "I can do all things through Christ which strengtheneth me."

For a season, self-focus, pride, and self-sufficiency shoved the little bits of Scripture I'd picked up from Dr. Peale's guidance into a mental lockbox as I tried to settle my conflicted mind. I'd remember the first half of Paul's assurance to the Philippians, "I can do all things," but would forget the second half, indeed the most important half: "through Christ which strengtheneth me." I took pride in my self-sufficiency, and ten years later I paid the price for it – I fell into a depression so severe I finally dragged my butt to a Christian psychological clinic and checked myself in as an outpatient. A week or two earlier, God had clearly spoken to me, directing me to open a faded, dusty Bible I hadn't had much use for during the prior 32 years. His message, planted directly into my heart, awakened me long enough to dial the clinic, set up the consultation, and check myself in. His Word saved my life. Literally.

It was during the weeklong evaluation, group therapy, and emotional vomiting that I became acquainted with God's Word in spades as a tool for mental, physical, and spiritual recovery and healing. It was then I was introduced to the Apostle Paul's urging in his letter to the Romans, "Therefore, I urge you, brothers and sisters, in view of God's mercy, to offer your bodies as a living sacrifice, holy and pleasing to God – this is your true and proper worship. Do not conform to the pattern of this world, but be transformed by the renewing of your mind. Then you will be able to test and approve what God's will is – his good, pleasing and perfect will" (Romans 12:1-2). Fifteen years later Eric Owings, Marc Owings' brother, slid up behind me during the first night of the Fully Alive retreat and slipped me a tiny piece of paper folded in half.

I'd just experienced a life-changing out-pouring of God's mercy as I tore open my chest and confessed to twenty-five men my brokenness, my anger, my fears, and my desperate search for my life's redemption from the death grip of past failures. I sat, shaking, yet covered over with peace and love and... relief. I unfolded that slip of paper and saw Eric had written a Scriptural citation: *Romans 12:1-2*. The very same verse given to me at the clinic. I've since had that citation tattooed on my right shoulder under an old rugged cross surrounded by all the junk I've laid at its foot. It's truly my life verse.

After that experience I dived headlong into the Word of God. Our church small group did a study reinforcing the power and practicality of absorbing God's Word through conscientious memorization and recitation. Like Ezekiel, Jeremiah, and the Apostle John, I ate it up! "When your words came, I ate them, /" wrote the prophet Jeremiah. "They were my joy and my heart's delight, / for I bear your name, / LORD God Almighty" (Jeremiah 15:16). I committed to starting each day by reading a devotional and its associated Bible verses. After all, Jesus started His day in private prayer: "Very early in the morning, while it was still dark, Jesus got up, left the house and went off to a solitary place, where he prayed" (Mark 1:35). Jesus didn't do anything until the Father directed Him. Likewise, I try to start my day with an attitude of open-mindedness and flexibility. I find I still approach my quiet time with my own agenda in mind, and sometimes as something to just check off my to-do list. But the more I humble myself before the sovereignty of God, the more and more I'm coming to understand why Jesus did what He did so early in the morning. The existence of this book testifies to my willingness to open myself up to God's direction through prayer and total absorption in His Word.

In the Apostle Paul's letter to the church in Ephesus, he commanded the Ephesians to "put on the full armor of God, so that you can take your stand against the devil's schemes. For our struggle is not against flesh and blood, but against the rulers, against the authorities, against the powers of this dark world and against the spiritual forces of evil in the heavenly realms. Therefore put on the full armor of God, so that when the day of evil comes, you may be able to stand your ground, and after you have done everything, to stand. Stand firm then, with the belt of truth buckled around your waist, with the breastplate of righteousness in place, and with your feet fitted with the readiness that comes from the gospel of peace. In addition to all this, take up the shield of faith, with which you can extinguish all the flaming arrows of the evil one. Take the helmet of salvation and *the sword of the Spirit, which is the word of God"* (Ephesians 6:11-17, emphasis mine). In Paul's metaphorical suit of armor, all the elements are defensive save one: "the sword of the Spirit, which is the word of God."

God's Word is powerful and fully alive! It's like the Force in the *Star Wars* movies. I remember Obi Wan Kenobi's words to Luke Skywalker after Obi Wan rescued him from the Sand People and brought him back to his dwelling: "The Force is what gives the Jedi his power. It's an energy field created by all living things. It surrounds us and penetrates us; it binds the galaxy together."[5] Except God's Word is real, penetrating us through the soul to the spirit, spirit to Spirit, binding not only the galaxy together but the universe.

"For the Word of God is alive and active. Sharper than any double-edged sword, it penetrates even to dividing soul and spirit, joints and marrow; it judges the thoughts and attitudes of the heart" (Hebrews 4:12). God's Word is a divine light saber!

Two years ago I had a particularly bad day wrestling with myself and with God about whether or not I should quit my job to pursue this writing vocation. I cracked open my notebook and wrote, "What is my greatest fear? Why am I so afraid to quit my job right now and pursue a full-time writing career?"

Under that question I began to write a bulleted list of all my reasons, starting with excuse number one: *fear of being poor*. God thwarted that lie with Jeremiah 29:11: "'For I know the plans I have for you,' declares the LORD, 'Plans to prosper you and not harm you, plans to give you hope and a future.'" That was followed by *fear of failure, resulting in becoming poor*. God stepped in and chopped that one into bits: "I can do all things through him who strengthens me" (Philippians 4:13 NRSVCE). Next I listed *fear of disappointing my father*, to which he threw three verses at me: Jeremiah 32:38, Galatians 4:7, and 2 Timothy 2:15. The list grew: *fear of not providing for my family, lack of confidence in my capability to actually do this job, fear of rejection by others who may think that what I did (quitting such a good-paying, secure job) was stupid.* One-by-one God revealed the lie in each one of the devil's flaming arrows by flea-flickering me a Scriptural reference to tackle each one. The common thread of all of these lies was lack of trust in God, but He showed me the defense of this potentially incapacitating lie as well:

> *Trust in the LORD with all your heart*
> *   and lean not on your own understanding;*
> *in all your ways submit to him,*
> *   and he will make your paths straight.*
> – Proverbs 3:5-6

He also revealed to me Job 42:2 and Philippians 1:6.

Whew! No wonder the psalmist rejoiced in God's precepts, God's statutes, God's Word. It's pure joy! And it's all free for the asking! In Psalm 119, the psalmist boiled down the wisdom of following the Living Word of God:

> *How can a young person stay on the path of purity?*
> *   By living according to your word.*
> *I seek you with all my heart;*
> *   do not let me stray from your commands.*
> *I have hidden your word in my heart*
> *   that I might not sin against you.*
> *Praise be to you, LORD;*
> *   teach me your decrees.*
> *With my lips I recount*

all the laws that come from your mouth.
I rejoice in following your statutes
    as one rejoices in great riches.
I meditate on your precepts
    and consider your ways.
I delight in your decrees;
    I will not neglect your word.
                    — Psalm 119:9-16

Hide God's Word in your heart (in other words, memorize it) and I guarantee you'll witness the amazing transforming power the Word of God will bring about, including filling your heart — and your life — with living joy.

CHAPTER 3
JOY IN WISDOM

When we walk with Him, we learn His ways, His wisdom, His love, and His boundless joy.
— Matthew Kelly, *A Call to Joy: Living in the Presence of God*[6]

Minutes invested in praying for wisdom will save days spent in overcoming mistakes. To advance in joy, first retreat with God.
— Tommy Newberry, *The 4:8 Principle: The Secret to a Joy-Filled Life*[7]

Hannah's a competitive gymnast, spending over 20 hours each week training in the gym. Because of this major time commitment, Mary and I had to chunk our tentative vision of Hannah attending public school and heartily embrace the new world order of home schooling. Yes, we're *those* kind of parents! This unconventional lifestyle has challenged us to not only choose an appropriate curriculum, but to establish consistency and discipline in teaching, and it has rewarded us with witnessing Hannah's joy in learning. She loves school – loves it! – especially math and drawing, and it tickles us when she absorbs phonics and applies it to both her reading and writing. The girl's already written and illustrated a book!

One morning I took over the educational duties while my Proverbs 31 wife scooted off to work. Part of Hannah's curriculum involves learning a new Proverb each week, and this particular morning the lesson was Proverbs 10:5: "He who gathers crops in summer is a wise son, / but he who sleeps during harvest is a disgraceful son." You know, Aesop's old "Ant and the Grasshopper" fable.

"What does 'wise' mean, Dad?" Hannah asked.

"It means to be filled with wisdom."

"But what's wisdom?"

"It's, uh, it's, well, it's the application of knowledge," I replied. Of course these are some big words and even bigger concepts for a fifty-year-old, uh, I mean, a five-year-old. "It's like when we learn something new," I tried to explain, "then we use what we learned. That's wisdom."

But like joy, wisdom is one of those concepts I've struggled to wrap my arms around, and my response to Hannah's query left me unsatisfied. What is wisdom, really? What does it mean to be wise? What does it mean to have wisdom? And how can wisdom bring joy? "It's a gift from God," Mary answered when I asked my wife what she thought wisdom was. "And how can a gift from God *not* bring you joy? It's like patience in a room full of kids. It's a gift." My wife is a very wise woman.

According to Bible Gateway's dictionary of Bible themes, wisdom is "the quality of knowledge, discernment and understanding characteristic of God himself. True wisdom, seen in the ministry of Jesus Christ, is a gift of the Holy Spirit."[8] The author of the Deuterocanonical Book of Wisdom wrote:

> *For she is a breath of the might of God*
> *and a pure emanation of the glory of the*
> *Almighty;*
> *therefore nothing defiled can enter into her.*
> *For she is the reflection of eternal light,*
> *the spotless mirror of the power of God,*
> *the image of his goodness.*
>   – Wisdom 7:25a, 26 (NABRE)

Wisdom is the splendor of God, the brilliance of His character, the reflection of His holiness.

The first Proverb Hannah memorized as part of her curriculum was Proverbs 9:10, "If you really want to become wise, you must begin by having respect for the LORD. / To know the Holy One is to gain understanding" (Proverbs 9:10 NIrV). This first step to gaining wisdom is a common theme running throughout the Bible: "And he said to the human race, 'The fear of the Lord – that is wisdom'" (Job 28:28a). "The fear of the LORD is the beginning of wisdom; / all who follow his precepts have good understanding. / To him belongs eternal praise" (Psalm 111:10). "The beginning of wisdom is to fear the Lord" (Ben Sira 1:14a NABRE).

But if fear – or sovereign respect – of the Lord is opening the door to wisdom, how do we invite her in? All we gotta do is ask! "If any of you lacks wisdom," James wrote in his epistle to the twelve tribes, "you should ask God, who gives generously to all without finding fault, and it will be given to you" (James 1:5). Ask and you shall receive, as Jesus said, but ask with a reverent, expectant heart, and with thanksgiving.

Take King Solomon, for example. When God told him He'd grant any request Solomon asked for, he answered, "'Give me wisdom and knowledge, that I may lead this people, for who is able to govern this great people of yours?'" (2 Chronicles 1:10). He didn't ask for riches, treasures, and glory, but for wisdom. In reply, God not only granted Solomon's request, but He also gave him the riches, treasures, and glory Solomon had left unspoken. Wisdom is more precious than anything, because "if riches are desirable in life, / what is richer than Wisdom, who produces all things?" (Wisdom 8:5 NABRE). Indeed, Solomon came to be known as the wisest (and richest) man who'd ever lived. "But seek first his kingdom and his righteousness," Jesus preached in Matthew 6:33, "and all these things will be given to you as well."

The writer of the Book of Wisdom described her this way:

Wisdom is radiant and unfading,
and she is easily discerned by those
    who love her,
and is found by those who seek her.
She hastens to make herself known to
    those who desire her.
One who rises early to seek her will
    have no difficulty,
for she will be found sitting at the
    gate.
To fix one's thought on her is perfect
    understanding,
and one who is vigilant on her account
    will soon be free from care,
because she goes about seeking those
    worthy of her,
and she graciously appears to them in
    their paths,
and meets them in every thought.
                    – Wisdom 6:12-16 (NRSVCE)

As I mentioned earlier, when God told me to write this book, my first reaction was one of surprise and disbelief. But then my faith gear kicked in and I told God, "Okay, this is Your deal. I'm a conduit for Your Spirit to work through me. I'll provide the fingers and the brain and the computer, but Your Spirit has to provide the rest." In other words, I needed Wisdom to show up at my gate in a hurry so I could complete my Daddy's assignment.

Later, while leading a Prayer Ministry training session at New River Fellowship, Denise

Bell, the Freedom Minister at the time, prayed over me. As she prayed she spoke this message to me: "You don't have to learn before you put pen to paper," she said. "You can learn while putting pen to paper." What Denise didn't know was I'd been spending a lot of time with my nose buried in texts in an attempt to understand joy. In this moment of prayer, Wisdom hastened to make herself known to me, and she's hung out with me throughout this entire adventure and beyond.

I'm constantly amazed when I revisit these chapters for honing and polishing and I read something I could not have possibly written on my own. "She understands the turns of phrases and the solutions of riddles," the author of the Book of Wisdom wrote in Wisdom 8:8b (NABRE). I continue to witness that truth first-hand, and it's amazing! It's in those moments I realize God's Spirit has been sitting here typing and whispering and enjoying this process right alongside me. I've provided the means, the Spirit has provided the inspiration, the words, and the "turns of phrase." As I've become vigilant to the Spirit's presence, my cares and worries about accomplishing what God assigned me gradually diminished to nothing. After all, I've got my very own Holy Ghost writer!

Once we acknowledge and respect God's sovereignty, and after we've asked Him to bless us with His wisdom, He'll make our paths clear and straight:

"Who has learned your counsel,
unless you have given wisdom

and sent your holy spirit from on high?
And thus the paths of those on earth were set
  right,
and people were taught what pleases you,
and were saved by wisdom."
                    – Wisdom 9:17-18 (NRSVCE)

For decades fear of failure, fear of financial disaster, and fear of man shackled me to the status quo. I was a slave to the comfort of the here and now, and I genuflected to the world's shaky promise of a secure future. Money and the accumulation of wealth had become my end-all be-all, despite its fickleness and empty promises. I rode the undulating roller coaster of the stock market with increasing distaste and distrust. I knew there was more to life, I just couldn't release the safety bar of the hope of future security and walk away from the never-ending vacillations of worldly living.

But once I began to sincerely trust God and embrace His wisdom, something miraculous happened: the light of God's face shined through the darkness of fear and illuminated the white stones of His promises He'd already placed on the path leading to Him. One-by-one things began to snap into place: God, through the wisdom of His Spirit, revealed the source and structure of this book; my company allowed me to transition to half-time employment, giving me time to begin this journey in earnest; the lady who moved in next door to us is a novelist and the co-owner of Progressive Rising Phoenix Press, my publisher; my company laid me off only two months before I intended to quit, and I received a generous severance package; opportunities to serve my fellow writers in the capacity of editor "just happened" to pop up – two opportunities in the same week – diminishing my fears about financial solvency as I continue to transition into full-time writing. God saved me – and continues to save me daily – with His wisdom.

And as dots connect and doors continue to open, as Wisdom pours into my heart and puts a smile on my face, joy walks hand-in-hand with her, and together they continue to reveal to me what's next. As Ben Sira wrote, "Whoever loves [Wisdom] loves life, / and those who seek her from early morning are filled with joy. / For at last you will find the rest she gives, / and she will be changed into joy for you" (Sirach 4:12, 6:28 NRSVCE).

CHAPTER 4

JOY IN TRUSTING GOD

Bring joy to your servant, Lord,
for I put my trust in you.
— Psalm 86:4

Maybe I'm a victim of selective memory, but I don't recall harboring very many cares in the world when I was a young child; as a kid I had seemingly unlimited opportunities to enjoy life, and my parents raised us with a liberality almost unheard of in today's society. Don't get me wrong, I fought with my brothers, instigated disobedience, and participated in wholesale stupidity. I was petulant, controlling, and I could be downright mean. When required, my parents could be strategic distributors of corporal punishment, from Mom yanking the back of my hairline to Dad snapping his well-worn belt against my bottom. But I knew my parents loved me and cared about me, even as I screamed "I hate you!" while opening and closing my bedroom door 100 times because I'd slammed it in a fit of anger. I trusted my parents to take care of me, even if I didn't realize it and appreciate it at the time, and in return, my parents trusted us.

During summer vacation my mom would shoo us outside after breakfast. "Get out of the house and get the stink blowed off you!" she would bellow. My siblings and I would rush through the screen door and tumble into fields and woods filled with bugs, mud, toads, snakes, adventure, and imagination. We spent hours exploring the forests, catching crayfish in the creeks, picking our way through the ruins of an ancient slaughterhouse we called "the barn," and climbing sheer cliffs rising from the creek bed to the crest of the hill facing our house. We built forts out of weeds, dams out of rocks, and go-carts out of scrap wood, tricycle wheels, and plastic Big Wheel tires. We rode our cool bicycles with high-rise handlebars, banana seats, and florescent orange flags ten miles on a busy state highway to a local swimming lake. We had all-out apple fights in the neighbor's side yard when the hard green apples hanging from the gnarled tree faded to pale yellow. And every afternoon, as the sun swept across the upstate New York sky and settled over King Hill, Mom would thrust her index finger and thumb into her mouth and whistle when supper was ready. I swear we could hear that shrill call a half mile away, and when the piercing sound reached our well-tuned ears, we immediately ran home.

My parents trusted us to entertain our-selves outside whether it was summer, winter, spring, or fall. They trusted us to keep our bearings, keep out of trouble, keep from killing ourselves (or each other), and keep playing. We trusted our parents to clothe us in bell bottoms, wide-striped shirts, jean jackets, knee socks, and Ked High Tops. We trusted Dad to go to work every day, come home, and kiss Mom as he walked in the front door. We trusted Mom to keep frying up liver, boiling up rigatoni, and cooking up venison roast for dinner. Joy was our agreeable playmate, and we took for granted the freedom of our parents' trust because that's all we knew as kids. Until I fell in love.

At twelve I started babysitting my brothers, ages ten and eight, and my four-year-old sister on Wednesday nights. Like a lot of good, dedicated Catholics, my parents dutifully drove into town to fellowship with other Catholics and non-Catholics alike at the church hall. In the century-old converted inn smelling of must and floor polish, one of the volunteers took a seat on stage promptly at 7:00 p.m., reached into the hopper, pulled out a ping-pong ball, and read off the first number: "B-4!" At which the crowd responded "And after!" My dad called Bingo while my mom hung out with the ladies and gambled the night away, all in the name of fun and raising money for the church, of course.

My babysitting responsibilities, like playing in the woods, were pretty simple: stay out of trouble, don't kill each other, and make sure everyone goes to bed on time. For this, and for doing my household chores, I earned 50 cents a week for an allowance. When I reached thirteen I started mowing our yard: $2.00 to push-mow the half-acre lawn, $1.00 to rake the cut grass, and 50 cents to collect the clippings and dump them on the compost pile. As the years rolled by and my hobbies grew more expensive, my parents declared that if I wanted to continue feeding my addictions I had to earn my own money. So over time I fell in love with not only airplanes and model rockets, but with money and its alluring benefits.

I worked hard for it. I kept a running tally of the income from all my 50-cents-an-hour babysitting jobs, adding it up constantly as I worked toward the goal of purchasing a new Sig R/C kit, another Estes rocket, or a Monogram model airplane. I soon gained a shining reputation as one of the most trusted babysitters in the Town of Maine, which swelled my tally sheet even more. Babysitting and lawn mowing led to frying grilled ham-and-cheese sandwiches and dishing up soft-serve at the local ice cream shop. I cleaned toilets, swept parking lots, and knocked down spiders from around the florescent lights illuminating the town's small grocery store complex. If I wanted something, I would set my financial goal and work my butt off to get it. At one time I worked three jobs to support my glider-flying habit while still a senior in high school.

I quickly learned that good hard work brought in cold hard cash, and cold hard cash bought what I wanted. And what I wanted brought me happiness. Sometimes. And sometimes at a price. As the Apostle Matthew wrote in his gospel, "What good will it be for someone to gain the whole world, yet forfeit their soul?" (Matthew 16:26). Halfway through college money began to edge into the spotlight of my striving as I chose to stick with engineering and table my desire to switch to journalism until after I'd earned my degree and secured a good-paying job. Then money became a third-rate means of redemption, an idol of second chances, the holy grail of my desires.

Slowly, insidiously, my trust in money and its false power to bring about the realization of my dreams overtook and replaced my trust in anything else. "Money is in some respects life's fire: it is a very excellent servant, but a terrible master," circus mogul P.T. Barnum said.[9] I believe him: my misplaced trust in money had turned my life into a regular three-ring circus, but not the fun kind. No, the kind featuring evil clowns, a freak show, and mistreated lions with mange.

In my quest to buy myself out of the hole of dissatisfaction I'd dug, I fell for every get-rich-quick scheme out there, setups like questionable multi-level marketing schemes, a militant goal-setting program on cassette tape, gold coins, penny stocks, the stock market, even my job. And with each failed attempt to make my quick million and move ahead with my writing career, God kicked out another pier holding up my fantasyland of trusting in money.

Isn't it ironic that "In God We Trust" is printed on every paper bill and etched on every U.S. coin minted in recent history? It should be a reminder that money is only a tool, a servant, a means to a greater end as long as it's framed in the proper perspective. But I didn't comprehend that truth; I built a road paved with the green stuff in all its fickleness, power, and empty promises.

The road I constructed meandered from greed to false hope to despair. It doubled back on itself, leading me from fear to depression to grief. It spun in ever-widening circles of mistrust in myself, other people, and, ironically, in money itself. I developed a deep disgust for people working in the financial industry because each one I'd ever dealt with had led me down a path of financial loss. And financial loss equated to loss of hope in the dream which tried again and again to germinate in my stony heart. I finally lost all trust in money while I watched in horror as the Great Recession swept away hundreds of thousands of dollars I'd saved over the course of my career.

As I writhed from the shock of the financial meltdown and its gut-wrenching effect on my 401K, and as frustration grew over the stagnation of my job's financial reality and potential, God propelled me into slaying my lust for money and convinced me to place my trust squarely in Him once-and-for-all. My love affair with the spirit of Mammon ended there. "And we know that in all things God works for the good of those who love him," the Apostle Paul promised the Christians living in first-century Rome (Romans 8:28). Not *some* things. Not *most* things. *All* things, both good and bad. And when God released me from the shackles of self-delusion and opened my eyes to the connectedness of the past and the promise of a joy-filled, prosperous future, I accepted His permission to step out in faith and step into His will. As King Solomon urged in Proverbs, I finally submitted:

Trust in the LORD with all your heart
and lean not on your own understanding;
in all your ways submit to him,
and he will make your paths straight.
— Proverbs 3:5-6

After years of false security and unfulfilled prom-ises, the spirit of Mammon finally spit me out. That's when God picked me up at Fully Alive, shifted my eyes away from the love of money and the bitterness of unforgiveness, and refocused them on His love, His abundance, and His security. "It is for freedom that Christ has set us free," the Apostle Paul wrote in his letter to the Galatians. "Stand firm, then, and do not let your-selves be burdened again by a yoke of slavery" (Galatians 5:1). In my new freedom I took off my yoke and relocated my trust from the burnt-out tenements of Mammon to the unlimited glory of the One Who created me. I was no longer a slave but a free man, and not only a free man but a son of the One True God. I found myself yoked to Christ. And it was good.

"Trust that I am right now creating these paths and opportunities for you," God had told me at the Fully Alive men's retreat in January 2011. "Enjoy and be filled with joy! This is the path." Like Abram trusting God's call in Genesis 12:1 to "'go from your country, your people and your father's household to the land I will show you,'" I took the leap of faith and began to trust. I mean, really deep-down-in-my-heart trust God and His promises.

But it wasn't easy. In fact, because of the decades of my reliance on money and the false hope of a secure future based on its sandy foundations, it took me another year to relinquish its hold, and still another year to jump feet-first into the river of trust. I divorced a steady six-figure income and the promise of a six-figure retirement to re-marry the One who "richly provides us with everything for our enjoyment" (1 Timothy 6:17). Like Abram did, I "went, as the LORD had told" me (Genesis 12:4). I'm still holding my nose as I'm being swept away from my old self by the stream of living water, but each "coincidence," each kiss on the cheek from God the Provider, each unexpected financial blessing inches me toward complete and total trust in the One Who "created [me] in Christ Jesus to do good works, which God prepared in advance for [me] to do" (Ephesians 2:10).

The psalmist wrote in Psalm 91:1-4:

Whoever dwells in the shelter of the Most High
  will rest in the shadow of the Almighty.
I will say of the LORD, "He is my refuge and my
  fortress, my God, in whom I trust."
Surely he will save you from the fowler's snare
  and from the deadly pestilence.
He will cover you with his feathers,

and under his wings you will find refuge;
his faithfulness will be your shield and
rampart.

God's faithfulness *is* my shield and rampart; He never gave up on me even when I gave up on Him. He never let me go even though I let Him go. He *does* hide me under His wings. The God Who created me and predestined me according to His plan "works out everything in conformity with the purpose of his will" (Ephesians 1:11). I can trust that "he who began a good work in [me] will carry it on to completion until the day of Christ Jesus" (Philippians 1:6). Finally submitting to God and trusting His will has changed my life forever. I trust myself again. I trust God again. And in that trust is an ever-abiding joy.

CHAPTER 5

JOY IN FEARING THE LORD

The fear of the LORD is the beginning of knowledge,
but fools despise wisdom and instruction.
— Proverbs 1:7

When I was growing up, I looked forward to Saturdays, not only for the morning cartoons, but for the afternoon monster movie matinees. My siblings and I would sit for hours glued to the TV, especially when the weather put the kibosh on romping around in four-foot-deep snow drifts, or hiking through the woods because it was pouring down rain.

I loved those old films like *The Crawling Eye, The Blob, Them, The Monolith Monsters,* and all the Godzilla movies. Especially the *Godzilla* movies! The theme of radiated monsters rang loud and clear back then, as the nation slogged through the Cold War, and the fear of nuclear annihilation hung like a pall of neutrons over our heads. We even practiced air raid drills in elementary school. My favorite movie at the time, however, had nothing to do with being vaporized by an H-bomb, but being scared to death by the ghostly skeleton of a woman dressed in a white wedding gown. I remember watching the 1958 classic, *The Screaming Skull*, at my friend Kevin's house one Saturday afternoon after a sleepover in their big, creepy, two-story house in the woods. Their property came complete with a graveyard hidden deep in the shadows of the backyard copse for added effect.

So on that fateful day, when the ghost of Marion, the murdered wife, appeared in snowy black-and-white on Kevin's television, I hid behind the sofa in utter fear until he somehow coaxed me out and convinced me to watch the rest of the flick. I don't know how I didn't wet my pants that day. But after recently renting *The Screaming Skull* through Netflix, and inviting Mary to watch it with me, I now know how campy, stupid, and poorly-acted that movie really was. Back then, however, it scared the bejeezus out of me! That, to me, was the definition of fear – plain, simple, and all-too-real. I don't remember spending many more nights at Kevin's house after that.

Thus began my initial confusion when I first started reading the Bible and came across the phrase "fear of the Lord." Fear of the Lord? Really? I mean, I feared screaming skulls, walking in the woods at night, driving in a blizzard, the crawl space in the basement, going to Confession, talking to a girl, reading out loud in class, and getting a B in a third-year engineering class, but fear of the Lord? I thought God was supposed to love me, protect me, and wrap me in peace and security; why should I be afraid of Him? It wasn't until recently that the true meaning of the term "fear of the Lord" came into the light – it was an "aha" moment that brought focus to my theological understanding of fear.

The Hebrew word for the noun "fear" in this context is *yir'ah*, which can mean both fear or terror *and* reverence or respect,[10] depending on the context. In Isaiah 11:1-3a, one of Isaiah's prophecies about the birth and ministry of the Messiah includes the noun *yir'ah* as one of the outpourings of the Holy Spirit:

A shoot will come up from the stump of Jesse;
   from his roots a Branch will bear fruit.
The Spirit of the LORD will rest on him –
   the Spirit of wisdom and of understanding,
   the Spirit of counsel and of might,
   the Spirit of the knowledge and fear of the
   LORD –
and he will delight in the fear of the LORD.
                  – Isaiah 11:1-3a

This Old Testament passage is the source of the seven gifts of the Holy Spirit (the "Spirit of the LORD"), of which the gift of "fear of the LORD" is stated then reiterated as something to be delighted in – to take joy in!

Likewise, in the New Testament, the Greek word for the verb "to fear" is *phobeo*, which also has a multi-faceted meaning: to fear, to frighten, or to be afraid *and* to reverence or to venerate.[11] And the Greek word for the noun "fear" is *phobos*, meaning fear or terror *and* (interestingly!) reverence for one's husband.[12] In his first epistle, the Apostle John wrote:

> *There is no fear in love. But perfect love drives out fear, because fear has to do with punishment. The one who fears is not made perfect in love.*
> −1 John 4:18

Because the fear John is writing about here is *phobos*, i.e., terror, this kind of fear cannot stand up to God, the Source of perfect love and perfect security. On the contrary, since perfect love drives out *phobos*, fear of just punishment is replaced by awe, wonder, reverence, and respect. This reverential joy, this fear inspired by redemption and fullness of relationship with God is the kind of fear God desires from His adopted sons and daughters. "Serve the LORD with fear," the Psalmist wrote, "and celebrate his rule with trembling" (Psalm 2:11a).

As I mentioned in Chapter 3, the first Proverb Hannah memorized as part of her first grade *My Father's World* curriculum was Proverbs 9:10, "If you really want to become wise, you must begin by having respect for the LORD. / To know the Holy One is to gain understanding" (Proverbs 9:10 NIrV). The NIV® translation says, "The fear of the LORD is the beginning of wisdom, and knowledge of the Holy One is understanding." And Psalm 111:10 echoes this proverb: "The fear of the LORD is the beginning of wisdom; all who follow his precepts have good understanding. To him belongs eternal praise." When we recognize our limitations, when we dismiss our flippancy and our pride, when we quit trying to use God as a genie to obtain our selfish desires, when we finally take God out of our little box and place Him back on His throne, recognizing His vastness, His infiniteness, His omnipotence, and His absolute sovereignty, *that* is fear of the Lord. And after this foundation of proper perspective has been established, only then can wisdom begin to grow in our hearts, and with wisdom comes joy.

Saint Thomas Aquinas wrote in his *Summa Theologica*: "If a man turn to God and adhere to Him, through fear of punishment, it will be servile fear; but if it be on account of fear of committing a fault, it will be filial fear, for it becomes a child to fear offending its father."[13] To put it another way, servile fear is the fear a slave has for his master, i.e., fear of punishment. Filial fear is the fear a son has for his father, i.e., a profound respect and reverence, but also a fear of offending his father because of his love for him.

I have to admit I spent a large part of my life as a slave to ignorance, living in servile fear of God's punishment. One of my deepest fears was dying in a state of sin and going to hell for even the smallest infraction. Every time I missed the mark, no matter how big or small, I logged the trespass in the massive filing system I'd built in my head until I purged it in a confessional. Then the mental filing would begin again the moment I pulled the curtain back and knelt in the pew to recite my penitential prayers. This continuous monitoring of my current state of sinfulness diminished my energy and focus, impacted my health, and severely limited my experience of joy. In fact, this obsessiveness tended to morph into depression, which dragged me further into the pit of ineffectiveness for the Kingdom.

The thought of eternally treading water with the other banished souls in the lake of fire held me captive, compliant, and subservient to fear. This vision of hellfire and damnation I'd learned and accepted over the first four decades of my life motivated my actions much more than the truth of God's grace. Whether it stemmed from ignorance, immaturity, or just bad teaching, I never quite comprehended the true purpose for Confession until the toxicity of the build-up-and-dump pattern finally drove me into the arms of a Savior Who'd already forgiven all my sins, past, present, and future.

Somehow, in all the years of faithful churchgoing and religious education, I missed the point in the story about how God put on a flesh suit and emptied Himself out to show us the Father's love and take away our sins "once for all when he offered himself" as the final sin offering on the cross 2,000 years ago (Hebrews 7:27). Needless to say, this powerful and destructive mentality of working myself to exhaustion to remain in a state of grace and stay out of hell overshadowed my capacity to experience and express gladness. I didn't think about much else, and consequently I was not free to enjoy life.

Don't get me wrong, I acknowledge the reconciliatory truth of repentance and the healing power of confession, both spoken and unspoken. However, it wasn't until I began to experience the freeing power of God's Word and comprehend the truth of Jesus' sacrifice and the freedom it brought that my servile fear began to yield to filial fear, maybe for the first time ever, and joy again began to bloom in my life. "Come to me, all you who are weary and burdened, and I will give you rest," Jesus promised. "Take my yoke upon you and learn from me, for I am gentle and humble in heart, and you will find rest for your souls. For my yoke is easy and my burden is light" (Matthew 11:28-30).

Once I relinquished legalism, once I let go of my Pharisaic mindset, once the Spirit convinced me that, as an adopted son of the Most High God, heaven was indeed my destiny and eternal life my reward, the terror of hell gradually released its power and I became free to live the life God intended for me. "The Spirit you received does not make you slaves, so that you live in fear again," the Apostle Paul wrote to the Roman church, "rather, the Spirit you received brought about your adoption to sonship. And by him we cry, 'Abba, Father'" (Romans 8:15).

"Abba" is the Aramaic word for "Daddy," and once I let go of the terror of hell, I climbed up into my Daddy's lap with awe and wonder. My heart opened to faith and hope and God's continuous presence. With it came the potential and reality of the Spirit's fruits of love, joy, peace, patience, kindness, generosity, faithfulness, gentleness, and self-control. Because, as the Apostle Paul wrote in Galatians 5:23, "Against such things there is no law."

"The fear of the Lord rejoices the heart," Ben Sira wrote, "giving gladness, joy, and long life" (Ben Sira 1:12 NABRE). And as fear of the Lord brings joy and celebration to our hearts, "the LORD takes pleasure in those who fear him, those who put their hope in his mercy" (Psalm 147:11 NABRE). Growing up in the Catholic Church, I experienced this fear in the reverential atmosphere of every mass, especially during the Easter Vigil and midnight mass on Christmas Eve. In those celebrations we sent our prayers and praises to the Father on the rise of incense and the lowering of eyes, in the solemnity of hymns and the hush of Eucharist.

I knew God sat on His throne, but at the time I didn't comprehend that I could "confidently approach the throne of grace to receive mercy and to find grace for timely help" (Hebrews 4:16 NABRE). It's no accident the three Synoptic Gospels record that, at the moment Jesus gave up His spirit, the curtain of the temple "was torn in two from top to bottom." (See Matthew 27:51, Mark 15:38, and Luke 23:45). This tearing of the curtain separating the Holy Place from the Most Holy Place – the Holy of Holies – symbolized the initiation of direct access to God (starting from the top) by anyone (ending at the bottom) through the blood sacrifice of Jesus, the atoning Lamb of God, because "without the shedding of blood there is no forgiveness" (Hebrews 9:22b).

Now I have no fear, no terror, no *phobos* of God's judgment because I have been bought for a price, and have been found blameless in His sight as I walk in His righteousness willingly given and humbly accepted. "For we know that our old self was crucified with him so that the body ruled by sin might be done away with," the Apostle Paul wrote in his letter to the Romans, "that we should no longer be slaves to sin – because anyone who has died has been set free from sin" (Romans 6:6-7).

The door to a satisfying, exciting, and joyful relationship with the Most High God can begin by letting go of the chains of slavery to servile fear and putting on the garment of filial fear. Only then can we bow our heads and open our hearts to the love, gifts, and promises of the One who deserves the focus of our entire being. As the Psalmist wrote in Psalm 33:8:

Let all the earth fear the LORD;
let all the people of the world revere him.

Alleluia!

CHAPTER 6

JOY IN WORSHIP

Come, let us sing for joy to the LORD;
let us shout aloud to the Rock of our
salvation.
Let us come before him with thanksgiving
and extol him with music and song.
— Psalm 95:1-2

One evening, Mary and I attended New River Fellowship's "First Sunday," a monthly night of worship and digging deeper into God's Word. An integral part of each service that evangelical churches like New River have in common is a half hour or so of praise, involving talented singers and musicians. Typically I listen to the music, sing the words... and let my mind wander all over the place. Even after eight years of attending non-denominational Christian churches, I still didn't fully get it. But that night something shifted. It's happened before, to a degree, but that night I lifted my hands above my head and closed my eyes during one song – and started crying. The Holy Spirit overwhelmed me. He poured into me, embraced me, loved me. Just for... me. I stood there, hands held high, and received His mercy, His love, His awesomeness. I opened myself up to Him and He gushed into me.

Moments later, the Spirit told me very clearly to pray for the guy in the chair in front of me. As we all stood and sang and danced and shouted, he sat with his face in his hands, virtually unmoving. So, in unquestioned obedience, I knelt down, put a hand on his shoulder, and prayed for him out loud. I don't know what was going on in his life, I don't know what he needed; the Spirit had nudged me to pray for him, so I did. And gosh it felt good!

The next morning I rolled out of bed before sunrise to take the dogs for a walk. I do my best thinking, praying, and creating in the quietness right before the neighborhood begins to stir, enveloped in nature's inspiration and God's whispers. The pre-dawn morning embraced me in stillness and mid-spring warmth as I led the dogs out the front door and onto the sidewalk. Something – movement, a flash of light, a disturbance – caught my attention, and I turned toward the western sky just in time to catch the green-white streak of a meteor sacrificing itself in the atmosphere for God's glory. It was truly a good-morning kiss from Daddy. Then I really noticed the sky: cloudless, black, painted with countless stars and the stroke of the Milky Way running southwest to northeast. The sliver of a waning crescent moon hung on the eastern horizon. The Milky Way glowed softly against the inky backdrop, more pronounced that morning than I'd seen in recent memory, reminding me of those photos you see from the Hubble telescope of nebulae and galaxies.

I walked with my face pointed toward the sky, barely glancing at the road, hardly checking to see if the dogs were still attached to my wrist. The old hymn, "I Surrender All," played over and over in my mind, accompanying me in a continuous loop as I walked in rapture and awe of God's glory. The flashlight was useless that morning; I truly walked by faith and not by sight.

God's creation increased in awesomeness, expanding my view of the unbounded vastness of the universe by the arm of an immense galaxy. I could feel God's presence, palpable, real, alive. I walked in peace, I walked fully loved, I walked aware of His Spirit, surrounded by God's infiniteness. *How could a God Who created all of this take the time for me?* I wondered. *But He does. He does!* A great horned owl called out a lonely hoot, hope cast into the darkness, waiting for a reply. A bullfrog harrumphed its own hope across a pond yawning in the pre-dawn stillness. I looked up into that depthless spiral of a billion stars and asked, "God, teach me how to worship You."

"This is how," He replied in my heart. "This is how."

To worship God is to express the deepest desires of our being for the Being Who created us. To worship God is to express the deepest respect and reverence for Him, to focus on Him with awe, to live for Him, to praise Him because He is Who He is: the Great I AM. "True worship is the acknowledgement of God and all His power and glory in everything we do," wrote S. Michael Houdmann. "Worship is to glorify and exalt God – to show our loyalty and admiration to our Father."[14] God breathed life into our spirit, soul, and body, and worshipping Him is the natural outflow of our desire to make Him our focus. God made us to worship. God created us to glorify Him.

The Apostle Paul wrote in his letter to the Ephesians, "For he chose us in him before the creation of the world to be holy and blameless in his sight. In love he predestined us for adoption to sonship through Jesus Christ, in accordance with his pleasure and will – *to the praise of his glorious grace*, which he has freely given us in the One he loves" (Ephesians 1:4-6, emphasis mine). And through the prophet Isaiah, God told the Hebrews, "'Bring my sons from afar / and my daughters from the ends of the earth – / everyone who is called by my name, / *whom I created for my glory*, / whom I formed and made'" (Isaiah 43:6b,7, emphasis mine).

Indeed, in the first of the Ten Commandments, God commanded the Israelites to worship only Him: "'I am the LORD your God... You shall have no other gods before me'" (Exodus 20:2,3). Our purpose in life is to worship God. He, in response, opens the door to unlimited and everlasting joy; we give Him glory, He gives us pleasure in worshiping Him. "But seek first his kingdom and his righteousness," Jesus said, "and all these things will be given to you as well" (Matthew 6:33).

One of my favorite Bible passages illustrating this truth is contained in the Gospel of Luke, chapter 10. As Jesus and His disciples traveled to Jerusalem for the last time before Jesus' death, they stopped at the home of Jesus' friends, Mary and Martha. There, while Martha busied herself preparing and serving the meal, her sister did absolutely nothing to help her. Instead, Mary sat at Jesus' feet, a position of reverence and respect – of worship – and listened to Him. Finally Martha had had enough: "'Lord,'" she said to Jesus, "'don't you care that my sister has left me to do the work by myself? Tell her to help me!'" (Luke 10:40). I can imagine Martha, cheeks covered with flour, blowing a strand of hair out of her face and pointing at Mary with a wooden spoon, exasperated.

But Jesus did something extraordinary: He refused Martha's request. Instead, He replied, "'Martha, Martha, you are worried and upset about many things, but few things are needed – or indeed only one. Mary has chosen what is better, and it will not be taken away from her'" (Luke 10:41-42). Mary had found her true joy while Martha had relinquished her joy to the distractions, expectations, and assumptions of busyness. I can relate.

All my life I've had a tendency to seek approval through accomplishment rather than to embrace God's truth that I am approved just because I am His child. There's nothing else I need to do to deepen His love for me. Absolutely nothing. No works will make Him love me more. No additional prayers can entice Him to favor me any better. No amount of study, knowledge, or wisdom will cause Him to hold me any closer. He loves me as much now as He has ever loved me, and as much now as He ever will. But because I equate lack of action for laziness, I compensate by keeping busy, to the detriment of my relationship with my God and His people. Instead of sitting at His feet and just loving Him, I spend too much of my time and energy trying to win His approval. This is not what God intended when He created us. "'Be still,'" the Psalmist wrote in Psalm 46:10a, "'and know that I am God.'" Be still in His presence. And worship.

When we turn away from the "better part" and shift our attention to the distractions of the world, we put ourselves in danger of worshiping something other than God; we become idolaters. Like the Hebrews worshipping the golden calf, or the Pharisees worshipping their manmade layers of rules, we shift our natural desire to worship away from God and toward anything that distracts our attention and energy. The love of money may be the root of all evil, but the worship of God is the beginning of all life. God made us to worship – and we will worship – but only worshiping the better part brings us true joy.

What does God want from us when we worship? He wants us. "Therefore, I urge you, brothers and sisters, in view of God's mercy, to offer your bodies as a living sacrifice, holy and pleasing to God – this is your true and proper worship," the Apostle Paul told the church in

Rome (Romans 12:1). In view of God's unde-served gifts – His mercy – the only true and proper worship is to offer our lives to the One who created us. He wants every bit of us, even our distractedness. "'For I desire mercy, not sacrifice, / and acknowledgment of God rather than burnt offerings,'" God told the Hebrews through Hosea (Hosea 6:6). And as we slough off our Martha busyness and put on our Mary rever-ence, joy is the natural outflow of our actions.

As I researched this book, I found that, by far, the majority of instances of the word "joy" in Scripture are within the context of worship, praise, and celebration of God. The Psalms espe-cially attest to joy in worship as David and the other psalm writers sang God's praises and released God's joy in their hymns. Worship leads to joy, and joy leads to worship. "But may all who seek you / rejoice and be glad in you, /" wrote David, "may those who long for your saving help always say, / 'The LORD is great!'"(Psalm 40:16). "Worship is aligning our mind's attention with our heart's affections," said Michael John Clement, Worship Pastor at New River. "Praise is the language God gives us to communicate with Him. Worship is the action. Let us sit back and watch God be God." Yes... let us watch God be God.

One morning, as I lay in bed praying, I told God, "I really don't know how to worship."

"Yes you do," He assured me. "You're doing it now. You're trusting me." I may not "get" wor-ship fully yet. I may stand unmoving in church except for the pumping of my right leg to the beat of the Sunday morning drums. I may look around in wonder at the folks who jump and wave their arms and shout at the ceiling, eyes closed, tears streaming down their cheeks, the ones who truly get it and are not just putting on a show. I may not worship out loud in my prayer language or wave my Holy Spirit fingers in the air. But, as Mark Driscoll, Pastor of Mars Hill Church in Seattle, wrote: "Worship is not merely an aspect of our being, but the essence of our being as God's image-bearers."[15] We worship because we're made in God's image, we pour out because God pours in. Our life is one of continuous worship; it's what we do, it's who we are.

King David described in Psalm 22:3 that God is holy, "enthroned on the praises of Israel." God dwells in the praises of His people! God's presence is real in the hearts of those who exalt Him. I may not get worship fully yet, but as I continue to walk in His presence, even on a dark road with the Milky Way spilling over me, as I reach up to give myself to Him with hands open to receive, He opens my heart a little more with each encounter. And who knows, maybe someday you just might see me turning cartwheels in the aisles at church, too.

CHAPTER 7
JOY IN REDEMPTION

... for as the weight of our sins was removed from our shoulders and we were taught to hope in the joy of eternal life... It is this joy of redemption and this hope of eternal life that have elevated and completed our happiness as human beings.
> – Matthew Kelly, *A Call to Joy: Living in the Presence of God*[16]

But I trust in your unfailing love;
  my heart rejoices in your salvation.
I will sing the LORD'S praise,
  for he has been good to me.
> – *P*salm 13:5-6

I met Jason Hoffman during the Fully Alive men's retreat in Lake Fork, Texas, in January 2011. One of the first things I noticed about him, besides his lanky stature and his curly reddish-brown hair, was the sincerity of his testimony and the heartfelt passion with which he delivered it. He leaned forward in his chair and spoke to the circle of men with the voice of a man convicted: weary, yet determined to get the burden off his chest. His eyes, red with emotion, implored us to listen to his story. And in that testimony I witnessed the power of repentance, confession, and forgiveness. In that testimony I got to see the genesis of a new life, one that even now glows with an almost continuous ear-to-ear smile, an aura that marks him as a man reborn, a true son of God. During that weekend, when Jason humbly surrendered his heart to God, God set him free.

Jason, a Certified Registered Nurse Anesthetist, had come from a broken home – his parents had divorced when he was young, and his mom worked three jobs to make ends meet. Because of the instability of his family life and his mother's virtual abandonment due to her work load, Jason inevitably got into serious trouble. At thirteen he embarked on a long spree of incarcerations, starting in juvenile detention facilities and working his way up to adult centers. As his life spun out of control, he wound up with two felony convictions by the age of nineteen.

But by the grace of God, he managed to turn his life around despite those two felonies. "Anyone with felony convictions isn't supposed to be licensed in the medical field," he later told the New River staff during a videotaped interview, "and He saw to it I was able to do just that."[17]

But instead of being grateful for what God had done for him, Jason instead focused on acquiring things and accumulating money, to the detriment of his relationships, his marriage, and his happiness. "I ended up broken," he admitted, "in so much pain, full of shame, full of guilt, full of pride."[18] Because his heart had become so hardened, he didn't believe he could ever climb out of the pit of shame. "I didn't think that I could ever be free."[19] And that's when the Spirit urged him to attend the Fully Alive men's retreat.

When he joined together with the other men at the retreat, when he confessed his brokenness, when he dropped his pride, fell on his knees, and gave himself over to God's mercy and offer of reconciliation, "my heart began to fill with the love and grace of Jesus, and I began to change. I began living the life once again that I didn't think was possible."[20] But, for Jason, it was not only possible, his absolute transformation from brokenness to redemption to true joy was nothing short of miraculous.

Today Jason recognizes his call to live righteously, to be a "spiritual man of God, and proclaim it, and own it, and share it with others."[21] Jason's story is a true testament to the power of redemption, salvation, and reconciliation, and the joy he now wears like a comfortable jacket makes him a bold and effective witness for God's Kingdom.

"The best day of my Christian walk was when I read Romans 12:2," he told me later. "Letting go of my worldly possessions, not caring about my position at work, how big my paycheck was, how big my house was, the car I drove, the clothes I wore, how much I had in savings, how many toys I had... My life changed, my relationship with the Lord changed, my faith changed, my attitude changed, *everything* changed!" And it shows. One day while at work a woman walked up to him and asked him flat-out, "What's the source of your joy? You're always happy."

"I simply answered, pointing up," he responded, "and said 'It's all Him.'"

Jason's story is a testimony to God's power, desire, and willingness to redeem our hearts from the grip of hell and the enticements of our fallen society. Redemption – the deliverance of mankind from the power and consequences of sin through the life, death, and resurrection of Jesus Christ – is, of course, the heart of the Gospel message. Salvation is the hinge pin of Christian faith, the purpose for the incarnation, the climax of the resurrection, mankind's history merging with His Story, the fulfillment of His promises. Indeed it's the reason why we're called to be a light for the world, why we need to set our lamps on the hill and not under a basket – the Gospel is, indeed, the Good News!

Salvation guarantees eternal life, but more importantly, redemption through Jesus' blood opens the door to accepting an intimate relationship with the Creator. "For the grace of God has appeared that offers salvation to all people," the Apostle Paul wrote in his letter to Titus. "It teaches us to say 'No' to ungodliness and worldly passions, and to live self-controlled, upright and godly lives in this present age" (Titus 2:11-12).

Salvation is ours, free for the asking. We just need to step out and ask!

Marc Owings, founder of elevateHim Ministries in Fort Worth, told me, "I believe this: When you receive Jesus Christ as Lord and Savior of your life, you're totally restored, totally redeemed. When we first acknowledge Him as Lord, then salvation comes." A person can receive that redemption, however, but not necessarily the freedom they'd hoped for. "I see people who have a portion of forgiveness," continued Marc, "they've been forgiven but they're not free. Forgiveness comes instantaneously. Your freedom you have to fight for." In other words, to become totally free and experience the fullness of joy that forgiveness and redemption bring, the redeemed heart has to sincerely believe in and embrace the transformation. Instead, many believers continue to wallow around in the mire of their past failings; they're redeemed... and totally miserable. To become free, we have to believe what God says in His Word is true.

"Redeemed is a special word for me, because of where I came from," related Marc, who grew up wild, unrestrained, and always looking for the next thrill, party, or fight. "The heavy voice and belief systems, the old tapes that played in my head told me there was no possible way I could be redeemed. What I came to believe and receive at age forty or so was that I *was* completely redeemed, that God does not judge me based upon my behavior but rather through the eyes of grace." When we get our hearts wrapped around this timeless Truth, we can begin to receive what God freely gives: forgiveness, freedom, and joy.

"Whoever is set free with Truth is free indeed!" Marc continued. "It's us looking in the Word for truth, believing it, and receiving it." The enemy of the past is at war with the blessings of the present. The fight is ongoing, the outcome imperative. To be free, to live in the joy of true freedom, is to press forward, no matter what. "Forgetting what is behind, pressing on, and running the race, not being easily entangled with sin that easily entangles us," said Marc. "Jesus is saying your sin doesn't nullify, it doesn't disqualify, none of those things. *That* is the joy of the Lord! No matter how bad I stumble and fall, He's with me. He says He'll never forsake you. There's incredible joy when we ponder that. But we let the cares of this world suck the joy out."

"If a man tells you something," he went on to say, "if you receive it from a man, then the devil can certainly talk you out of it. But once you hear the Father say 'Marc, you're redeemed,' the bottom line at the end of the day, no matter what, is... I'm redeemed. Totally brand new." There is joy in this revelation, and according to Marc, "That's what spurs us on."

And once our eyes are opened to this truth, nothing can stop us from bearing witness and building up the Kingdom of God on earth. "When you have an epiphany or revelation of joy," Marc explained, "I believe it's one of the most dangerous weapons for the enemy, because it's louder than a sermon or a song, and you can see it from a distance, which reflects back to the Scripture 'You will be a light on a hill.'"

A few years ago Mary's mom, Janet, gave me a Christmas present, a three-foot-long, six-inch tall plaque that says, "Live in such a way that those who know you but don't know God will come to know God because they know you." I hung that plaque at the foot of our cross wall in the living room. It's true: Jesus called us to bear witness to His Truth, and as we joyfully carry out our calling, people will come to God; this is what it means to live the Gospel. As Jason Hoffman witnessed when the woman stopped him and asked, "What's the source of your joy?" all we need to do is point up. And nod with a knowing smile.

"Whoever has been forgiven much, loves much," Marc Owings said. "In the case of Jason Hoffman, he went to the deeper depth of his past than most people, where God plunged him to the depths of His love in a greater way, and when he came out, all of us sitting there at Fully Alive realized he had just come from the depths of God. Freedom, forgiveness, love, and truth, it was evident. All he could do was cry. His eyes never turned off all weekend. And he wasn't crying for joy himself, but as I watched him, he was also crying and weeping in joy for other people. Once you've been there, there's no going back."

"It is for freedom that Christ has set us free," the Apostle Paul wrote to the church in Galatia. "Stand firm, then, and do not let your-selves be burdened again by a yoke of slavery" (Galatians 5:1). Approaching the throne of grace without shame, confessing, repenting, and receiving in our hearts the forgiveness freely given opens the door for God's healing to transform our lives from one of slavery to sinfulness to the freedom of redemption. And once we are freed, we are freed indeed! "For, 'Everyone who calls on the name of the Lord shall be saved'" (Romans 10:13, Joel 2:32).

"It's not what He saves us *from* – He saved us *for* joy," declared Sharon Grissom, one of our life group facilitators and an incredibly strong faith warrior. In Psalm 106, the psalmist asserted, "Yet he saved them for his name's sake, / to make his mighty power known" (Psalm 106:8). God saves us *for His name's sake*, so that we'll not only continue to rejoice in Him, but so that we can glorify Him with our lives! He restores us for the relationship, forgives us to declare His mighty works, redeems us for love and for joy.

"The glory of God is a human being fully alive; and to be alive consists in beholding God," said St. Irenaeus of Lyons.[22] And only by embracing the truth of our redemption and the complete forgiveness of our sins – past, present, and future – can we begin to fully glorify God by living out the life He created for each of us. "Believe and receive what has already taken place," said Marc Owings, "instead of letting the rearview mirror – the past – dictate your future." Live fully alive! Live fully in joy!

CHAPTER 8

JOY IN GRATITUDE

Joy is the fruit of appreciation.
        — Matthew Kelly, *A Call to*
        Joy: Living in the Presence of
        God[23]

And whatever you do, whether in word or deed,
do it all in the name of the Lord Jesus, giving
thanks to God the Father through him.
        — Colossians 3:17

One Saturday afternoon Mary kicked Hannah and me out of the house so she could host a baby shower for a neighbor. Because we hadn't visited her Grandma and Grandpa in a while, I decided to head up to New Fairview, Texas, to help Mary's dad work on his 1926 Ford Model T coupe. The trip takes about an hour, but it can sometimes seem like five, depending on Hannah's level of engagement and the mood I'm in. Some days a road trip can be fun, other days I'd rather pawn her off to the Leapster GS, or play the "Quiet Game" for the whole hour (which she actually does well at, by the way!).

The instant Hannah hears my seatbelt click into place, one of two phrases invariably rolls out of her mouth: "Dad, can I have a piece of gum?" or "Dad, let's play the _____ game," filling in the blank with a selection from the made-up-game library in our heads. At that time, we had quite an extensive collection: "Tell Me a Story, Dad," "Sing Me a Silly Song, Dad," "The Rhyming Game," "What Machine Makes this Sound," "What Animal Makes this Sound," "What Shape is It," and "The Color Game" were some of her favorites. But the one game she loved the best was the "Let's Make Up a New Game Game."

So on that cool March afternoon, as we drove up the farm road toward the interstate, I managed to progress about three miles before Hannah asked, "Dad, can we make up a new game?"

"Yes," I sighed. "How about the 'Thank You God Game?'" I hoped that by immediately taking control of the situation I wouldn't be sucked into one of her imaginary games fraught with a myriad of ever-shifting rules requiring the Rosetta Stone and an Enigma cipher machine to decode them. That, and I'm a control freak.

"How do you play it, Dad?" she asked in her sweet little voice.

"Well," I answered, "you think of something you're thankful for and thank God for it."

"Okay," she said.

"I'll go first," I called. "Let's see... Thank You, God, for my job."

Hannah caught on instantly. "Thank You, God, for trees, because we can sit in the shade."

I continued, "Thank You, God, for our cars."

"Thank You, God, for heaven."

"Thank You, God, for my family."

"I'm thankful for dirt, so we can dig in it and play in it," Hannah said. "And I'm thankful for all the different colors. I'm happy for our whole entire planet, and I'm happy for our whole entire house, and for our whole entire neighborhood." She was even thankful for the floor in our house and for our church family!

And as we continued to play I realized something: my thank you's focused mainly on possessions, while her thank you's encompassed not only material objects, like our house and our dogs, but more subjective and sublime things such as her experiences, her spirit, her Creator and His Creations. I choked up when she said, "I'm thankful for my heart," and I sat in awe as I realized my then four-year-old daughter understood gratitude, thankfulness, and appreciation better than I did.

In those few minutes of imagination, her expression of pure gratitude revealed the difference between the junk-filled head of an adult and the Spirit-filled heart of a child – while I focused my thankfulness on "stuff," she focused her thankfulness on God and His gifts. Whew! Talk about a life lesson in the form of a 25 pound preschool kid! This experience helped to remind me, again, of the joy and freedom of just being thankful.

As I've mentioned before, one of the most influential books I've experienced is Norman Vincent Peale's *The Power of Positive Thinking*. To say this book has reset my perspective more than once is an understatement. I've read *The Power of Positive Thinking* more times than any other book I own, including, I confess, the Bible. If I was ever stranded on an island and had to choose only two books to keep as I washed ashore, I'd clutch the Bible in my right hand, and *The Power of Positive Thinking* in my left. This book helped form my perspective on the power of gratitude, the authority of God's Word, and the power of attitude and prayer to align heavenly will with earthly reality.

In one particularly memorable anecdote from the book, a 52-year-old man consulted Dr. Peale because he believed "everything he had built up over his lifetime had been swept away."[24] The man had let the "dark shadows of hopelessness"[25] distort his thinking. Dr. Peale challenged the man's wretched, self-defeating beliefs by taking out a piece of paper and writing down the values the man had left. With the pastor's prompting, the man ended up listing seven good assets he still possessed. When Dr. Peale shoved the list across the table, the man grinned and said, "I guess I didn't think of those things."[26]

The negative influence of what we've forgotten, or what we're taking for granted, can kick the piers out from under the foundation of what we remember, experience, and actually possess. Whenever I'm facing a challenging day, or when my mind wanders down the dark path of self-pity or negativism, or when I'm walking the dogs around the neighborhood at 5:30 a.m. immersed in my thoughts and the Holy Spirit's loving whispers, I often just start thanking God for anything and everything that pops into my mind, challenging myself to play the "Thank You God Game" for 45 minutes straight. Believe me, it can quickly put things into perspective. You'd be amazed at the smallest details your soul can conjure to be thankful for! And you'd also be amazed at how such a simple prayer of gratitude can quickly turn your mourning (or morning) into joy!

As I write this chapter, Thanksgiving is only three days away. As coordinator of the after-school program for The Rock of Sports and Performing Arts, the gym where Hannah trains, Mary put together a curriculum of thankfulness and gratitude for the month of November. Mary felt called to help cultivate, and maybe even introduce, an attitude of appreciation for the everyday blessings we may take for granted. One of the projects she developed for the month was a "gratitude journal," where the kids answer a series of questions beginning with the preamble "What are you thankful for that's..." When asked "What are you thankful for that's small?" one of the girls in the program responded, "I'm thankful for how small my love for God is and [how] it will get bigger." Out of the mouths of babes, I'm tellin' ya!

"A thankful attitude opens windows of heaven," Sarah Young wrote in *Jesus Calling*.[27] The moment I wake up in the morning, I try to jumpstart my day by praying, "This is the day the Lord has made, I will rejoice and be glad in it, for I believe I can do all things through Jesus Christ who strengthens me." You may recognize my wake-up prayer as a combination of Psalm 118:24 and Philippians 4:13. I find that starting off the day with an attitude of rejoicing, thankfulness, and appreciation banishes negativity and instills joy in my heart from the get-go; this simple prayer can sweep away some powerful negativism. Mary wonders how I can be so happy immediately after the alarm buzzes and I roll out of bed. Now my secret is out!

In his first letter to the Thessalonians, the Apostle Paul wrote, "Rejoice always, pray continuously, give thanks in all circumstances, for this is God's will for you in Christ Jesus" (1 Thessalonians 5:16-18). Giving thanks in *all* circumstances is God's will for us, as is rejoicing (expressing joy), and praying (engaging God in conversation). Giving thanks when things are going well is one thing, but thanking God for the challenges and flat-out nasty stuff? That's an attitude-changer, a door opening to God's storeroom of unlimited joy. As the psalmist wrote in Psalm 100:4, "Enter his gates with thanksgiving and his courts with praise; give thanks to him and praise his name."

In his letter to the Philippians, Paul wrote, "Do not be anxious about anything, but in every situation, by prayer and petition, with thanksgiving, present your requests to God" (Philippians 4:6). The result of presenting our petitions with thanksgiving? "And the peace of God, which transcends all understanding, will guard your hearts and your minds in Christ Jesus" (Philippians 4:7). The fruit of thanksgiving is peace, a peace which goes beyond the natural and is anchored firmly in the supernatural.

Thankfulness raises the awareness of God's presence in my life, and with this awareness comes joy. Little things I may have passed by without noticing come into sharp focus in the light of the Great I AM: the delicate brushstroke of a hot pink sunrise between the hard gray horizon and a thick purple cloud layer, that flash of momentary radiance, God's "Good morning" as I finish up the day's devotional; the unexpected rain storm that pops up the day I write "Water trees" on my to-do list; the sudden discount on the hardwood flooring we'd been wanting to install, but didn't want to pay *that* much for; the inrush of sudden inspiration tumbling through my head at 3:00 in the morning, thoughts that perfectly complete the chapter I've been stuck on for the past couple days. When you embrace a moment-by-moment appreciation, God will play "Where's Waldo" with you all day long by hiding His little pleasures wrapped in good timing just to see you smile when you notice them. He's a great Daddy!

I like to think of these as "Thank You, Jesus" moments, where Mary and I just can't help but smile and say "Thank You" to the One who orchestrates our joy. And as gratitude becomes a habit, as I open my eyes to even the smallest things to be thankful about, I find myself saying "Thank You, Jesus" *a lot* during the day. What a great way to start it, what a fulfilling way to experience it, and what a spectacular way to end it.

One morning I woke up with my sinuses on fire and my throat irritated from the dry winter air. "That's one thing I don't like about this time of year," I complained to Mary as I stumbled out of bed. "The heater dries out my sinuses." Then instantly I said, "Thank You, Jesus, for the heater," and I imagined what it would be like to suffer through winter without a furnace in the house. As I sat on the bathtub step writing this experience in my notebook, Mary walked into the bathroom to get a shower. "Thank You, Jesus, for hitting my husband," she said. Believe me, I'm thankful He clobbers me over the head with these nuggets of inspiration – it makes my job all that much much joy-filled as I recognize the gifts He's poured out on me and my family.

Appreciating the gifts – and the Giver – makes having received the gifts even more valuable. When I was a kid, my mom made sure I wrote out and mailed off a thank you note for every birthday present, graduation gift, or Christmas present I'd ever received. I don't think I fully appreciated this expression of gratitude at the time, especially after a particularly large haul from a birthday or graduation party, but as I grew older I realized that writing out a thank you note by hand forces you to slow down a bit and actually reflect on the giver's thoughtfulness, and maybe even sacrifice. The act of expressing appreciation can make the gift all that much sweeter and more memorable – to this day I can remember specific wedding gifts Mary and I received, and who gave them to us. Now we hover over Hannah for days as she writes out her thank you notes in halting first-grade script, and it warms my heart to see the enjoyment she receives in doing it herself.

Gratitude raises my capacity to receive and express appreciation for even the smallest things, tangible or not. As I practice gratitude, I look forward to finding the little pleasures God sprinkles throughout the day for me to find, pecks on the cheek from the One Who wants me to experience life with joy, peace, freedom, and gratitude. Thank You, Jesus, for good health. Thank You, Jesus, for financial provision. Thank You, Lord, for opportunities. Thank You, Jesus, for my talents and abilities. Thank You, Daddy, for my family, my friends, my church, and my relationship with You. And thank You, Jesus, for the opportunity to glorify You by living today as You intended, with a heart of gratitude. May You implant this attitude ever deeper into our hearts. And, by the way, thank You, Lord, for You!

CHAPTER 9
JOY OF A CHILD

A great man never ignores the simplicity of a child.

— fortune cookie

People were bringing little children to Jesus for him to place his hands on them, but the disciples rebuked them. When Jesus saw this, he was indignant. He said to them, "Let the little children come to me, and do not hinder them, for the kingdom of God belongs to such as these. Truly I tell you, anyone who will not receive the kingdom of God like a little child will never enter it."

— Mark 10:13-15

Being a dad has opened my eyes to a plethora of truths, but three points in particular stand out: 1) children have a natural propensity toward joy, 2) it's okay to have fun and enjoy life, and 3) boogers can be considered a sixth major food group. Okay, I'll admit the third point may be a stretch for most of us above the age of twelve, but if you really want to know what joy is, if you truly desire to embrace joy and live life filled with trust, wonder, mystery, fun, curiosity, and simplicity, embrace Jesus' challenge to "receive the kingdom of God like a little child."

My daughter is a walking guidebook to what joy looks like, and every day she proves God has an unfathomable sense of humor. Hannah demonstrates the Kingdom of Heaven in living color, and her innocence, playfulness, trust, and ability to live in the moment have effectively chipped away at my rigidity, OCD, and caring what others think about me. Her giggle is enough to chase away demons of self-pity and anger, and her constant singing replaces them with angels of calmness and clarity.

Art Linkletter, prolific author and motivational speaker, was best known for the segments on his early television show *House Party*, where he asked kids questions and got back candid and sometimes hilarious responses. Mary and I have discovered since Hannah's birth that we have our very own "House Party" every day; how can you not when you've got a natural-born comedienne tugging at your heart and lifting your spirit?

The girl makes us laugh, from her perpetual silliness (mostly eruptions of random noises, whistles, and eardrum-busting squeals while imitating various animals, especially guinea pigs) to her rabid independence when dressing herself (in leopard-print tights, polka-dot sweater-shirts, and neon-glowing socks, all at the same time) to her spontaneous creativity with Elmer's School Glue, construction paper, Scotch tape, and imagination. But what continuously amazes us is her capacity to sling hysterical one-liners that can sometimes outdo the best stand-up comedians. If a sense of humor is a sign of intelligence, Hannah's IQ must be over 200.

One evening I sat at the kitchen bar while Mary finished prepping sides for dinner. The grill was heating up outside and I was waiting for her to give me a nod so I could throw on the steaks. Suddenly we heard a knock at the front door. Hannah ran from the foyer into the living room, announcing someone was here. By this time Mary and I had become proficient at identifying fake knocks from real ones, so Mary hollered, "I'm not opening the door for anyone, except the Christ!"

Hannah scampered back into the foyer, turned around and declared, "Yep, it's Jesus, all right!"

One afternoon Mary drove her sister, Laura, brother-in-law, Scott, and Hannah into Fort Worth to do some shopping in preparation for Laura's 50th birthday party. While in the Texas Christian University area they decided to stop and grab a bite of lunch at a Mexican restaurant. After they finished, Mary pulled the car onto the busy four-lane street with the intention of doing a U-turn at the next intersection, but after moving all the way over to the left-hand lane, she realized she couldn't pull a U-turn at that junction. She voiced her opinion of the situation loud enough for Hannah to hear, and Hannah quickly defused the situation: "Mama," she said, "I'll keep an eye out for cops while you do a U-turn." Hannah was four at the time.

As I mentioned, one of the most valuable lessons I've learned from raising a child is that it's okay to have fun in life. Having a child gives you all sorts of excuses to act like a kid again. For instance, our whole family still goes trick-or-treating with the neighborhood at Halloween. We go to the theater to watch kids' movies, and we take Hannah to the circus once a year. She thinks we go to the circus mainly to eat cotton candy an hour before bedtime. We ride the kiddie rides at fairs and theme parks, and we play all sorts of board games, from *Chutes and Ladders* and *Candyland* to *Parcheesi* and *Sorry*. Hannah learned how to play the *Star Wars* edition of *Monopoly*, after acing her *Monopoly Junior* game. We search for bugs. We go on twilight toad hunts. We play Putt-Putt. But all too fast she's growing up and losing her little-kidness one eye roll at a time. It makes me sad, but it also makes me realize I don't have to let go of fun even if Hannah seems to be growing out of the more juvenile stuff. We all have the capacity – and freedom – to hold on to that childhood sense of wonder, mystery, playfulness, and joy. Indeed, we have the obligation.

When Hannah was about two, a wadded up sheet of paper and a cardboard box could hold her attention for hours. For her it wasn't the gift that mattered, but the box it came in. Mary and I prayed she'd never outgrow her fascination with paper products, as they were much cheaper than Barbie dolls and so much easier to obtain; who'd have thought a toilet paper tube, a ball of yarn, and a glue stick could be so fascinating and versatile? Alas, her taste in toys has become more sophisticated as she's gotten older (she's into Legos now), but our joy in watching her toss aside the toy to play with the wrapping paper opened our eyes to the capacity of a child to find mystery in even the simplest things.

We could all learn a lesson in this truth, as God has set before us a world of paper wads and cardboard boxes called "life," and if we look at it through the eyes of a child, His infinite mystery can turn the ordinary into the extraordinary. Life, in all its wonder, can provide unlimited joy to those who seek the Lord with childlike faith and the capacity to take every situation and turn it into a double-sided puzzle.

"Jesus is an essentially happy man," John Eldredge wrote in his book, *Beautiful Outlaw: Experiencing the Playful, Disruptive, Extravagant Personality of Jesus.* "He loves life. How could the joy of the Lord be our strength if the Lord is seldom joyful?"[28] And how can we be the light for others if we cover up our own light with gloominess, complaining, and just plain seriousness? "We are the people of God," said Amy Hossler, a member of New River Fellowship, reflecting the theme of Psalm 126:2. "And if people don't see joy in us, are they going to want what we have?"

When Hannah was three we spent a week at Disneyworld in Orlando. Each day we visited a different theme park, from Epcot Center to Animal Kingdom to Hollywood Studios, and each day Mary helped Hannah gather autographs from the various Disney characters we spotted. But one character in particular eluded us: Mary Poppins, Mary's favorite. On the last day of the trip, we took the ferry boat across the lagoon to Magic Kingdom and set out to explore Cinderella's castle, ride the Dumbo Flying Elephant ride (I barely fit), and watch the parades.

As the morning grew hot we found our way to the merry-go-round where my wife finally spied her hero. Mary Poppins stood alone in front of the carousel, wearing a white Victorian dress with red bodice, and topped with a white silk hat tied around her chin. She carried her signature umbrella. Mary squealed like a little girl, abandoned Hannah and I, and ran to Mary Poppins with arms outstretched, clutching the autograph book and the pen. In that moment my wife shed 25 years and reaffirmed to me her continued capacity for wonder and enjoyment. I couldn't get a word in edgewise for fifteen minutes after she said goodbye to the magical nanny! What a joy!

Joy is freedom, and playfulness is the offspring of freedom. And if freedom begets playfulness, playfulness begets invention. Mary laments she doesn't know how to play. She generally hands activities like drawing, making up ridiculous songs, and telling stories over to me. She has a hard time playing a game Hannah created on the fly because she has little patience for the invented rules, lack of rules, or fluidity of rules. Me? This is one area I'm happy with just going with the flow. I play by Hannah's made-up rules even if they make no sense whatsoever.

For instance, Hannah asked me one day if I'd play a game with her, and when I agreed, she proceeded to open the bottom drawer of our entertainment unit and pull out a pack of cards, five dice, and three bean-bag juggling balls. Hannah then laid out three cards face down between us. Next, she threw one of the bean-bag balls onto the line of cards, flipped over the card the ball had landed on, then rolled the five dice until a combination of one, two, or three of them added up to the number represented by the card. When it did, she picked up the card from the floor and set it beside her; this was a card she'd won. Then it was my turn. Surprisingly the rules remained intact as we continued to draw cards, throw balls, and toss dice, and when Mary called us for dinner the smiles on our faces proved both of us had won the game.

Children teach us flexibility and the ability to employ spontaneous imagination. One afternoon Mary and I watched Hannah put on a ballet demonstration in the middle of the living room floor. She showed us the plié and the grand plié, followed by various numbered ballet positions. Watching this precocious five-year-old's little body flowing with her own internal rhythm and joy brought tears to my eyes. She got hung up on ballet position #3, but instead of letting frustration stop her, she pursed her lips and said, "I'll just make it up." So she started with #1, flowed into #2, made up #3, and moved directly into #4. I couldn't speak for the longest time, even to tell her how proud I was of her. Mary found her voice before I did and praised Hannah for her beautiful demonstration. All I could do was nod in agreement.

Like I've said before, kids have one foot on earth and another in heaven. I'm convinced Hannah feels the pulse of heaven continuously, and she lives, moves, and has her being in a joyfulness that definitely defies circumstances, like when her daddy's being grumpy or her mama's being impatient. When it comes to joy, Hannah is the teacher and we world-weary adults are the students.

If only we beat-down adults could take it to heart and live the same way, wouldn't life be so much more fun? So filled with joy? So much less serious and more heaven-like? Joy in playing, in making up stories, in camping out in the back yard after gorging ourselves on s'mores. Joy is in drawing and sculpting Play Dough creatures and building forts out of bar stools and blankets. Joy convinced me I need to let go of fear and follow God's calling to write – I'm in the sweet-spot of my experience, and Hannah is a catalyst for creativity, goofiness, and just plain having fun. "Through the praise of children and infants / you have established a stronghold against your enemies, / to silence the foe and the avenger," King David wrote in Psalm 8:2. What a better way to slap the devil silly than to belly laugh with a kid?

Jesus Himself said the Kingdom of God belongs to the children, or those who become child-like, not in immaturity and ignorance, but in wonder, trust, faith, and love. In His day, children were widely considered to be second-class citizens in many cultures, so placing a child amongst Jesus and His disciples could have been construed as offensive. No wonder the disciples rebuked the people when they brought their kids to Him. But Jesus was in the business of being offensive, peeling away layers of legalism to expose the underlying truth to free His children – all of His children – from the oppression of religiosity and the destructiveness of sin. Allowing little children to be brought to Him illustrated God's unconditional love regardless of age, affluence, or social status. It also provided Jesus a moment to instruct those listening in the eternal benefits of embracing playfulness, spontaneity, trust in the Father's providence, imagination, creativity, and joy.

These are the keys to heaven, both here on earth and in our legacy beyond. Art Linkletter died in 2010 at age 97. He'd made a career out of imagination and interacting with children. I'm convinced he knew the secret to joy. "I've been around long enough to develop some insights," he told the *Orlando Sentinel* in 2007. "Don't retire, become a 'seniorpreneur,' keep a positive outlook, and maintain your sense of humor."[29] Amen, brother Art. Amen!

CHAPTER 10
JOY IN OUR CALLING

We don't do this for the money. We do this because we love it. The rest will follow.
— Amanda M. Thrasher,
author and publisher

For the LORD your God will bless you in all your harvest and in all the work of your hands, and your joy will be complete.
— Deuteronomy 16:15b

On a cool evening in early November, Mary and I invited Pastors Scott and Renee Crenshaw over to our house for grilled steaks. After we finished dinner and enjoyed our slices of homemade Granny Smith apple pie slathered with equally homemade vanilla ice cream, I asked Scott, Senior Pastor at New River Fellowship, if he considered himself living out his calling. To me it was a rhetorical question; it was pretty obvious by the joy he exudes.

"I think so," he responded, smiling and stroking his goatee. "I really do."

I nodded. You see, I'd been struggling mightily with my calling for years, not so much in figuring out what my calling was – I knew exactly what it was – but with stepping out and answering that calling with a trust in God deep enough to pull the ejection handle on my tech job and parachute into a new career in writing. I truly wanted to live out Goethe's imperative, "Whatever you can do or dream you can, begin it."[30] I'd only been at this writing thing full time for three months when I asked Scott the question. The man obviously loves his job, and his spot-on sermons, his animated delivery, and his love for the flock he pastors reflect the passion and joy he wears.

"I was duck hunting one time," he told me. "It was freezing cold, I mean, it was miserable! We got out there in the boat and we turned the heaters on, and we got some poor dog sitting on the floor of the boat waiting to dive into the water. And so we're sitting there, and all throughout the morning, in the freezing cold, the water almost turned to ice, I'm hearing this sound, this *thump-thump-thump-thump-thump,* and I'm thinking 'There must be an oil pump or something somewhere around here.' Finally I realized it was that dog. His tail was thumping. What was he excited about? He was excited about the moment when the guy goes 'Cut 'im!' and the dog dives out into that freezing cold water. But that's what he's made for." The Pastor laughed.

"So, at the end of the day, I'm petting the dog and I noticed his tail was literally bloody. And the first thought that came to my mind was, 'God, that's how I want to be.' I call it bloody-tail passion. I said, 'I want to live in that.'"

I want to live in that... Gosh, who doesn't?! I want to be so caught up in fulfilling God's will for me that I sit in the bottom of the boat, tail thumping, just waiting to explode with a bark of delight to scatter the ducks of joy all over Creation. So many people just exist, merely moving through life joylessly, cowering like a beat dog, or floating around like a piece of driftwood on life's ebb and flow. They never discover their calling, or worse, they know it but never pursue it. They don't do anything differently. Like zombies they go through the motions, dead but undead, losing body parts like hearts and souls along the way. "Those who cannot remember the past are condemned to repeat it," philosopher George Santayana once said.[31] Those who cannot remember their passions or what moved them or what brought joy to their hearts stand condemned by their own false truths. They slog along in a parade of fools led by that king of lies: worldly security.

One of my deepest fears was reaching the end of life, looking back on not only what I'd accomplished but also the opportunities I'd passed up because of terror, and saying, "So what the hell was that all about?" Rockford E. Toews, in his essay "One Less Accountant," wrote, "Rather than purposefully living, the vast majority of people's lives are little more than a series of reactions to events and forces outside themselves. That's not truly living. That's just survival. Yet most people willingly engage in simple survival today in the belief that they will get their chance at actual living tomorrow. If they can earn enough money now surely they will be able to retire one day and enjoy life."[32]

Jesus said as much in the Parable of the Rich Fool:

> *And he told them this parable: "The ground of a certain rich man yielded an abundant harvest. He thought to himself, 'What shall I do? I have no place to store my crops.'*
> *"Then he said, 'This is what I'll do. I will tear down my barns and build bigger ones, and there I will store my surplus grain. And I'll say to myself, "You have plenty of grain laid up for many years. Take life easy; eat, drink and be merry."'*
> *"But God said to him, 'You fool! This very night your life will be demanded from you. Then who will get what you have prepared for yourself?'*
> *"This is how it will be with whoever stores up things for themselves but is not rich toward God."*
> *– Luke 12:16-21*

Let me ask you something: Do you believe God wants you to actually enjoy the work He's lined up for you instead of being miserable in the job you've lined up for yourself? Do you believe God has a plan for you, a gift of purpose tailor-made just for you, a vocation to live out with excitement, joy, and, dare I say, *fun* that will leave you breathless with wonder at the end of each day? Do you believe God doesn't intend for us to spend all of our energy chasing a dollar, but instead He intends for us to spend all of our energy chasing Him?

And let me ask you this: If you didn't have to worry about money, what would you be doing with your life right now? If you could have the ultimate dream job, what would it be? I pray you're actually doing what you love right now, but if you're not, I hope your answer to these questions brought a little thrill to your heart, a little shot of adrenaline, a little hope to your weary fingers and strained eyes. Because if you're living out God's calling – His will – for you, you *don't* have to worry about the money; in fact, you don't have to worry about anything! "But seek first his kingdom and his righteousness, and all these things will be given to you as well," Jesus said during His Sermon on the Mount (Matthew 6:33). Not a few of these things, not some of these things, but *all* these things will be given to you as well.

From the very beginning of my corporate work experience, and even while attending college prior to entering the 9-to-5 world, I realized not many people actually enjoyed doing what they were doing, but they kept doing it anyway. During my almost thirty year stint in the corporate workforce, I heard countless gripes, complaints, and lamentations from folks about how much they loathed their jobs. They lived the

Dilbert comic strip every day, but without the punch line. I saw how their jobs were making them sick, lethargic, unmotivated, grumpy. I saw, in other cases, how their jobs were killing them. "Why don't you just quit?" I began to ask in response to these moans. "Because I need the money," came the invariable answer. And so these folks kept right on griping, complaining, and lamenting. It stunk.

"Command those who are rich in this present world not to be arrogant nor to put their hope in wealth, which is so uncertain," the Apostle Paul cautioned in his first letter to Timothy, "but to put their hope in God, who richly provides us with everything for our enjoyment" (1 Timothy 6:17). Notice how Paul said "*everything* for our enjoyment." Everything. For our *enjoyment*! God is the God of provision and unlimited resources. But for decades I went right along with those folks complaining about their jobs yet doing nothing about it.

Oh, I may not have complained much out loud; I tried to wear a more positive attitude on the exterior. But I could definitely relate to the complainers, the whiners, and the bellyachers. I felt trapped between maintaining a lifestyle I'd built up over the years and remaining miserable, or finally believing what God says about provision, protection, and doing His will, and risk living... joyfully. "Men and women of faith struggle rather to surrender to and trust God and His providence," wrote Matthew Kelly in *A Call to Joy*. "This surrender and trust free Christians of worry and anxiety and allow them to focus their energy on the realities of the present moment."[33]

I knew God never meant for our work to suck the life out of us like a spider draining the blood from a bug and leaving the husk to shiver in the wind. Over the years I'd allowed myself to be brainwashed by the mantra of retirement planning, until I realized that no one – no one! – in the Bible ever retired. Shoot, Moses was, what, 120 years old when he finally died? Just imagine if he'd turned in the key to the Hebrew executive washroom at age 65 and continued to hang out in the desert with Zipporah, cultivating succulents for a hobby. Where would the Jewish people be? Probably still in Egypt, serving the Egyptians as they'd done for over 400 years prior to Moses stepping in and demanding Pharaoh to let go of his people. No, Moses started his main career at age 80, after 40 years of gaining experience living in the desert. Noah started building the ark when he was something like 500. Abraham didn't even have Isaac until he was 100. Dang, in Biblical perspective, I'm just getting warmed up!

Dan Rasmussen is the Campus Pastor for New River Mineral Wells, in Mineral Wells, Texas, but before his life in full time ministry began, Dan was a chiropractor. Son of a church planter, pastor, missionary, and jack-of-all-trades, Dan went to college after high school, not for ministry, but for football. After he met his wife, Janna, and they started dating, football suddenly became much less important. Dan and Janna got married while he was a sophomore in college. "My thought then was, 'how am I going to provide for this woman?'" he told me.

"Part of my upbringing was always helping those in need," he said. "Watching my parents, and seeing their hearts, I wondered if I could find a career that helped those in need as well. I began searching healthcare professions and landed on a career in chiropractic." After graduating from chiropractic school, Dan started his own practice. At first "it was great! I was my own boss and 'living the dream,' or at least I thought I was." After struggling for five years, "the business was sucking the fun and joy right out of me."

So, after praying and discussing the situation with Janna, Dan walked away from his practice and began working for a friend in sales, "but it still was just a job," he said. "A means to pay my bills." Again he began to question what he was doing, and then his friend let him go from that job as well.

"Soon after we moved to Mineral Wells we began attending a traditional church and realized there weren't many younger families there. We were really bothered by this." So falling back on his desire and ability to fix things, he and Janna started looking into how they could reach younger families with a meaningful church experience. "After a lot of prayer, research, and meetings," Dan continued, "we were approved to start a new 'contemporary' service in the gym. It was my first taste of real ministry and I absolutely love it." Despite opposition against this church service, it grew. "We knew that God had ordained these steps for us to take, and we took them. It was the first time I felt like my life had a purpose. I was finally able to scratch the itch. I was like a fish that had been flopping around on the shore, gasping for oxygen, and finally finding water."

Dan and Janna moved away from that church after a year and a half, but the service they established continues to this day. Then God led the couple to plant another church in Weatherford, Texas. "Church planting is the hardest, most thankless job," explained Dan, and yet it's "the most rewarding and exciting job all the same. I love everything about church planting. Once it's in your veins, it's hard to get out." As they drove back and forth between Mineral Wells and Weatherford, Dan and Janna realized God had planted them in Mineral Wells for a purpose, so after New River proposed opening a campus in their town, New River hired him as the Campus Pastor there.

"I love doing what God has called me to do. It is awesome knowing that you are at the center of His will. I love sharing the love of Jesus with people who are so far away from it, to see people who are broken in so many ways become healed and whole again." One of Dan's favorite Bible verses is Philippians 2:1-4, a passage which greatly expresses his ministry of service and compassion. "My joy," he said, "comes from serving the One Who is the glue that unites us all, and gives our lives purpose. Where He guides, He provides. He makes my joy complete."

"For we are God's handiwork," the Apostle Paul wrote in his letter to the Ephesians, "created in Christ Jesus to do good works, which God prepared in advance for us to do" (Ephesians 2:10). Notice what Paul said: God prepared our good works *in advance* for us to do. "All the days ordained for me were written in your book, /" the Psalmist wrote in Psalm 139, "before one of them came to be" (Psalm 139:16b). God's will, His calling on our lives, was ordained even before we took our first breath.

Dan Rasmussen followed his heart of service first to the medical field, then to sales, and each time his heart yearned for more. His intentions were right, but at first the vehicles were wrong. God finally removed him from those vehicles and placed him into full-time ministry. And He has made good on His promise of Philippians 4:19: "And my God will meet all your needs according to the riches of his glory in Christ Jesus." Dan is living out his bloody-tail passion. With a passion!

Jesus said to His disciples, "'Whoever wants to be my disciple must deny themselves and take up their cross and follow me. For whoever wants to save their life will lose it, but whoever loses their life for me will find it. What good will it be for someone to gain the whole world, yet forfeit their soul? Or what can anyone give in exchange for their soul?'" (Matthew 16:24-26). Are you forfeiting your soul? Or worse, are you ignoring your calling, trading it in for a life of comfort and security rather than excitement, purposefulness, and joy? For the sake of pure joy, it is your imperative to seek God's will, find His calling on your life, and dare to step out and live it with all your heart. Because life's all about bloody-tail passion, and I don't know about you, but I want to have the bloodiest!

CHAPTER 11
JOY IN SERVING

Do not forget to show hospitality to strangers,
for by so doing some people have shown
hospitality to angels without knowing it.
– Hebrews 13:2

I often traveled to Buffalo, New York, for my engineering job, and from November through April the work occasionally gave me the opportunity to re-experience one aspect of life growing up in the Northeast: cold and snowy weather. And western New York in the winter can deliver some of the coldest and snowiest.

During this particular trip, the Delta Airlines MD-88 on which I flew transitioned into the Buffalo-Niagara International airspace on a quiet February afternoon, with temperatures hovering around freezing. In any given year the area gets about 94 inches of the white stuff, and during February the typical monthly total is just under two feet. But this particular year the snowfall totals had been significantly lower. So as the jet skimmed over the dairy farms and neatly-packed suburbs on approach to the airport, I noticed the area was not blanketed by snow as expected, but covered in the flat brownness of a worn-out winter. Threads of discolored slush huddled in the shadows of the naked woods, and dirty piles of it stood hunched around the perimeters of parking lots.

That night the thin cloud deck drifted out, unveiling a crisp full moon, setting the stage for temperatures to fall below freezing. The next morning when I peeked out the hotel window I saw the cars in the parking lot covered by a patina of crystalline frost. Lucky for me, the rental car I drove came equipped with an ice scraper. Unfortunately, not all rental car companies ensure their customers leave the airport with this critical piece of hardware. After leaving the hotel and starting the Ford Fusion, I attacked the ice on the driver's side window. That's when I noticed the car next to me was running, steam wafting out of the tail pipe, windshield wipers occasionally stuttering across the ice-covered windshield. The driver, a young woman, tall and bundled in a long coat, swung open the door, rushed out of the car, and hustled into the hotel.

Well, that ain't gonna cut it, I thought, continuing to skin the Fusion of its coat of rime. Obviously the young lady didn't have a scraper, and I wondered if she'd run back into the hotel to see if she could borrow one. At that moment I determined I would scrape her windows when I finished mine. *What better opportunity to do a kind deed for someone?* So after I finished the Fusion, I started scraping off the windshield of the young woman's car. Suddenly the passenger side door opened and another young lady peered over the car roof. "Thank you," she beamed. "Thank you so much!"

"No problem," I replied, and kept scraping. The first woman hustled back down the sidewalk from the hotel entrance toward the car, hands in the pockets of her long coat.

"Thank you," she called as she climbed back into the driver's seat.

"You're welcome," I answered. "I saw your windshield wipers moving and I thought 'That ain't gonna cut it.'" I worked my way around their car from the driver's side windshield, around the back, and finishing on the passenger's side windshield. The passenger cracked her window to again express her appreciation. "Are you going to the airport, or going to work?" I asked.

"We're going to take the bar exam," the woman replied.

"Awesome!" I said. "God bless. You're both going to do well!" After saying goodbye, I climbed back into my car with a smile on my face, a light in my heart, and joy in my spirit. That felt good! Really good! And as I pulled out of the parking lot and headed to work, I actually choked up with joy: a kind deed, even something as simple as scraping ice off someone's car windows, had made my day. Literally. I thought of the verse in the Bible where it says to be kind to strangers because – who knows? – you may actually be serving angels (Hebrews 13:2). To me, those two ladies were angels because they provided me an opportunity to serve, even if it seemed insignificant.

The rest of the day I was charged up – I worked with confidence and assertiveness, and with a clarity and alertness that lasted the whole shift. *Man,* I thought, *if doing a simple kind deed does this, I need to keep my eyes open for every opportunity I can find!* What a disproportionately huge reward for such a simple act.

Fred Chapman, a fellow church member, and an active volunteer for Kids Against Hunger, invited volunteers to show up one late afternoon at the distribution facility on the west side of Weatherford, Texas. The goal that evening was to load two trailers with enough bags of food to provide over 100,000 meals for people in Mexico. I jumped at the chance to bring Hannah along to participate in this roll-up-your-sleeves service project. She squealed with excitement and anticipation.

After we arrived at the distribution center that hot summer evening, I set Hannah to one side and told her to stand clear of the line of volunteers wheeling out pallets of boxes. The workers passed box after box, bucket brigade style, from the pallets to the trailer. Each box contained a dozen bags of rice and soy mixed with vegetables, vitamins, and minerals. Hannah never complained as she watched, despite the glaring sun and shimmering heat. "Are we volunteering, Dad?" she asked.

"Yes we are, Sweetie," I assured her, sweat dripping off my forehead. "This is what we do. We help each other."

After we finished stacking boxes in the trailers, and the crew distributed the loads evenly over the axles, the volunteers hugged and said goodbye to the drivers as they started their long overnight journey to the border crossing into Mexico. Fred then picked up Hannah and visited with her for a few minutes, holding her and talking to her eye-to-eye. Hannah smiled and nodded, perfectly comfortable in the arms of this strong leader who still exudes continuous joy despite experiencing tragedy several years ago. Knowing Fred, he poured as much encouragement and excitement into Hannah about serving as I had, maybe even more. I then collected my daughter and whisked her off to get a dish of ice cream for a job well done. "When can we volunteer again, Daddy?" she asked as we headed to Chik-fil-A.

"We'll have lots of opportunities to do this again," I assured her.

"Yay!" she cried. Her joy in volunteering is just getting started, but for that day, her joy was complete.

On one occasion an expert in the law stood up to test Jesus. "Teacher," he asked, "what must I do to inherit eternal life?" "What is written in the Law?" [Jesus] replied. "How do you read it?" [The expert] answered, "'Love the Lord your God with all your heart and with all your soul and with all your strength and with all your mind'";

and, "'Love your neighbor as yourself.'" "You have answered correctly," Jesus replied. "Do this and you will live."
                    – Luke 10:25-28

When God handed down the Law through Moses to the entire assembly of Israel, He commanded, "Love your neighbor as yourself" (Leviticus 19:18). When the law expert tested Jesus, Jesus turned the question back on the questioner by asking him how he read the law; his reply was accurate. "Do this and you will live," Jesus said. Yes! Your heart will be glad. Your face will be radiant. You'll walk in God's light, God's energy, God's communion. You'll walk in joy!

In John 13:34, Jesus gave the disciples a new command: "Love one another. As I have loved you, so you must love one another. By this everyone will know that you are my disciples, if you love one another." By His death, Jesus brought the Law to fulfillment, but loving one another transcends the Law as Jesus transcended death. Jesus' command – this new command – placed the Father's imperative to love our neighbor as ourselves in the context of Jesus' ministry among us: we love one another because He first loved us.

Jesus' ministry cleared away the religiosity blinding us to the Father's true nature. Jesus walked the earth to demonstrate, in the flesh, God's glory, meekness, power, love, and simplicity. Jesus served, and time and again throughout the gospels, He clearly demonstrated that, while redemption of mankind was paramount to His mission, service was the context in which that redemption and salvation was wrapped.

"For even the Son of Man did not come to be served, but to serve," He iterated in Mark 10:45. After He had washed the apostles' feet the evening of His arrest, Jesus asked the Twelve, "Do you understand what I have done for you?" (John 13:12). The King of kings and Lord of lords – the Creator of the universe and everything in it – had just put on the role of servant, stooped down, and washed their dusty, stinky, calloused feet. The teacher had lowered himself to serve the students. Why?

"You call me 'Teacher' and 'Lord,' and rightly so, for that is what I am. Now that I, your Lord and Teacher, have washed your feet, you also should wash one another's feet. I have set you an example that you should do as I have done for you. Very truly I tell you, no servant is greater than his master, nor is a messenger greater than the one who sent him. Now that you know these things, you will be blessed if you do them" (John 13:13-17). We will be blessed if we do them. We will be blessed as we look up to our Savior and God and follow His example of service, love, and humility.

With both of us working, Mary and I sometimes struggle to keep the house in a relative semblance of order. For two perfectionists living out our Spiritual gift of administration, being able to write "I Love You" in the dust covering the dresser, or watching the clumps of dog hair chase each other around the living room floor when we flip on the ceiling fans stretches our tolerance for disorganization to the edge.

One of my pet peeves is piles: unfolded laundry piled for days in the clothes baskets on the cedar chest; stacks of Hannah's artwork perching on top of the jewelry case; mountains of unread mail heaped on the kitchen bar ready to slide into my quiet-time space like the slipping of a tectonic plate.

Mary has little tolerance for unwashed dishes, especially when the strata of plates, silverware, and cooking utensils leaning over the sink provides archeological clues as to what we ate two days ago. "I wish we had a kitchen fairy," Mary once complained. Unfortunately, neither Whirlpool nor GE manufactures those, but we discovered that we do indeed have one.

One morning after showering, I walked out of the bedroom into the kitchen to fix breakfast. As I rounded the corner I saw Hannah standing on her blue plastic step stool in front of the sink, singing. She scrubbed a plate with a soapy wash-cloth while water streamed from the faucet. "Good morning," I greeted, not wanting to startle her.

She turned and smiled at me, brown eyes bright with excitement. "I'm the kitchen fairy, Daddy!" she declared. "I'm washing dishes before Mom gets up." Talk about melting my heart! Here stood my six-year-old with sleeves rolled up, dish in one hand, washcloth in the other, happily serving her Mom without being asked. She saw a need and jumped in with no complaints, but with determination and birdsong and a happy smile.

Hannah loves serving with Mary and me on Sundays in the church nursery. In the "Yellow Room," we get to hang out with a dozen or more one and two-year-olds still in diapers. Hannah proudly wears her "Leader" badge around her neck, and she enjoys reading to the kids, serving them Pepperidge Farm Goldfish at snack time, and supervising the wiggly children while they scribble on coloring sheets with drool-covered crayons.

"Why do you like to serve in the Yellow Room?" I asked Hannah one morning.

She thought for a moment, then replied, "I like putting the drawing paper down, helping with the snack, putting the chairs down. I like doing that."

"Why do you like doing that?" I prodded.

"Because it's fun!"

Yes! Because it's *fun!*

"Our kids are terrible about following our instruction," declared Pastor Scott Crenshaw. "But they're great at following our example." Give a child an opportunity to serve, and you get to watch Jesus in action, real-time. And, if you're like me, you'll end up learning from their example as much as they learn from yours.

I strive to live out the Apostle Paul's instruction to husbands in his letter to the Ephesians, chapter 5: "Husbands, love your wives, just as Christ loved the church and gave himself up for her" (Ephesians 5:25). I consider myself a servant husband – it gives me pleasure to serve my wife in any way I can, from cleaning the house to picking up Hannah from gymnastics to having dinner ready when she walks through the door at the end of a challenging day. Likewise, Mary lives out King Lemuel's description of a wife of noble character in Proverbs 31:

> *She is clothed with strength and dignity;*
> *she can laugh at the days to come.*
> *She speaks with wisdom,*
> *and faithful instruction is on her tongue.*
> *She watches over the affairs of her household*
> *and does not eat the bread of idleness.*
> *Her children arise and call her blessed;*
> *her husband also, and he praises her...*
> — Proverbs 31:25-28

There's nothing sexier than my wife mowing the lawn on the big red lawn tractor while sporting a white baseball cap and ear buds!

I took Hannah to the gym one Friday for acrobatics lessons, and after I sent her off with her instructor, I climbed up the bleachers to read my Kindle and watch her practice. Toward the end of the session, one of the gym moms mentioned something that prompted me to jump into the conversation: "Tomorrow morning we have to take Hannah to a birthday party," I said, "then we have to drive her to her aunt and uncle's house, then tomorrow night we're attending a wedding." Five women turned around simultaneously and stared at me.

"You know what your schedule is for tomorrow?" one of them asked.

"Uh, yes, I do."

"My husband is clueless," she told me. The other women nodded.

Another woman lamented, "My husband doesn't care what's going on." More nods.

"Yeah, mine's lucky to know what's happening today, let alone tomorrow or the next day," another wife griped.

Wow! Talk about an eye-opener! I can't be the only surviving servant husband in the world, am I? This dramatic reaction from these gym moms blew me away! "Thank you for being, as the ladies at work say, 'the most beautiful husband ever,'" Mary texted me one day. Beautiful? I receive that. I love responding to the privilege of being a servant husband; I'm designed for it! That's why I was put on this earth. I try to pay attention to my wife's needs, even if it's just to keep my mouth shut and listen and nod when she's venting. Even if it's just sweeping up dog hair or putting the chickens up for the night or bringing home a bouquet of flowers from Walmart and putting them in a vase before she gets home from work. Even if it's massaging her feet while we veg in front of the TV and watch the latest episode of *The Walking Dead*. As Anakin Skywalker said in *Star Wars Episode I*: "Mom, you said that the biggest problem in the universe is no one helps each other."[34] I don't want to reside in that universe, so I'll continue to live out my Christian walk with an attitude of service and love.

After all, that's what Jesus called us to do.

CHAPTER 12
JOY IN GIVING

All you need do is recognize that you have the ability to allow God to work through you and bring happiness to others. And the more you give happiness to others, the more you will have it for yourself.

— Matthew Kelly, *A Call to Joy*[35]

A couple months after I'd left my job, I started to feel the pinch of our severely-diminished family income while balancing the checkbook one day. The three-figure tally at the bottom of the check register did nothing to assure me I'd done the right thing giving up my generous income in exchange for the adventure of a writer's life. I scrutinized the debits — mainly birthday party expenses for Hannah — and felt my face flush.

A couple weeks earlier, Mary had sacrificed her own birthday and anniversary gifts in exchange for throwing Hannah a big sixth birthday party, and she'd busied herself buying candy for the piñata, purchasing gift bags for the party-goers, and putting down a deposit to hold the professional magician. On top of all that, we'd caved in to Hannah's persistent nagging for guinea pigs and ended up spending even more money on a cage and all the trimmings. And I knew Mary hadn't yet finished: she still had to buy an assortment of colored sand for one of the party activities.

For months Mary had been trying to convince Hannah to relinquish her obsession with the purple Fisher Price kitchen she'd played with since she was a toddler. She'd outgrown the thing by a year or two, but whenever we broached the subject of donating it to the church, she'd whine about still wanting to play with it. So there it sat in her bedroom, taking up space and collecting a fine patina of dust. But when we revealed the guinea piglets to her on her birth-day, we seized the moment to coax her into giving away the toy. "We need to make a space to put the cage," Mary told her. Mesmerized by the piglets, Hannah agreed.

The next morning Mary happily loaded the plastic kitchen into the back of the car and headed to the gym. After dropping Hannah off, Mary then drove to the church office and un-loaded the toy. She'd intended to head into Fort Worth to purchase the colored sand for the birthday party activity, but she ran out of time and returned to the gym to squeeze in a home-school session with Hannah between gymnastics training sessions.

While teaching first-grade addition, Mary offhandedly mentioned to the other homeschool moms that she hadn't been able to buy the sand she needed. Her intention was to make the 30-minute trip into town the next day. Michelle Lockhart, Hannah's gymnastics coach since she was eighteen months old, stopped what she was working on and looked at Mary. "What did you say?"

"I have to go to the Hobby Lobby in Fort Worth tomorrow," Mary repeated, "to buy colored sand so the girls at Hannah's party can fill dolphin key chains."

"Hold on one second," Michelle said. She dropped the paperwork she was organizing and called her husband, Heath. After chatting a minute, she hung up. "Heath will bring you a box of sand and dolphin key chains we just got from our church," she said. "They were throwing them out so we took them and brought them home last night. He'll drop them off today."

In that moment everything clicked: Mary had given Hannah's plastic kitchen to the church that morning, and a huge plastic bin filled with play sand and dolphin key chains arrived on our doorstep that afternoon. Jesus promised, in Luke 6:38, "Give, and it will be given to you. A good measure, pressed down, shaken together and running over, will be poured into your lap. For with the measure you use, it will be measured to you." That morning Mary had resolved to buy four different colored bags of play sand for about $10. She and Hannah then donated a toy not worth anything except to the hearts of the children who would now enjoy playing with it. That afternoon our family received more than *four dozen* bottles filled with different-colored sand. We gave, and God poured about $140 worth of sand and key chains into our laps. In fact, we used only what we needed for the party and returned the rest of it. Thank You, Jesus!

I love to give! In fact, it's one of my Spiritual gifts described by the Apostle Paul in Romans 12:6-8. And the joy I receive from giving is truly worth the sacrifice of giving; the joy of giving is itself the reward. As Jesus promised, those who give with the right attitude will receive back what they gave, and more. Jesus' allusion in Luke 6:38 refers to a basket filled with grain or flour that was first filled, compressed, shaken to settle it even further, then added to for good measure. A true abundance in return for a simple act.

Why do I give? First, I can't help myself! Giving is my calling, even when it hurts – the reward, for me, is in the giving. But I admit I also give because of God's promise to reward us in return. I have a heart of expectation, although what I receive may not be what I expected. God yells "Surprise!" to Mary and me a lot, and I'm completely convinced that because we faithfully and cheerfully donate our time, talents, and treasure, we've been blessed beyond blessed; God is glorified in our giving. The testimony alone is worth at least a few thousand denarii!

By choice and by our hearts' desire, Mary and I also tithe, the Old Testament tradition of giving the first 10% of our income, our "first fruits," to the church. We tithe to honor God, but we also tithe because, simply, it works as God promised. In Malachi 3:10, God threw down a challenge: test Him in this and watch what He does. Believe me, when you get your heart right, when you give cheerfully according to 2 Corinthians 9:7, when you drop dearth mentality, when you let go of greed, pride, selfishness, and fear, giving produces the sweet fruit of God's limitless abundance and "Praise Jesus" joy! You'll end up wanting to encourage everyone to give from their hearts as well!

I believe, however, that one hindrance to giving is the perception that God's blessings are poured out *only* in financial form; we give $100 to the church, we expect to receive a check in the mail or an injection into our bank account for 30, 60, or a hundred times the amount given, and when that doesn't happen, we crack the door open and allow discouragement to slither in and make its home in our hearts. God is not limited in how (or when) He doles out His good measure. The promise is that He *will* dole it out. God *does* want to prosper us. He *does* want to give us good gifts because He is a loving and faithful Father (see Jeremiah 29:11 and Luke 11:11-13), but God is not limited by our limitations, expectations, pride, selfishness, or idolatry. As God spoke through Isaiah: "'For my thoughts are not your thoughts, neither are your ways my ways,' declares the LORD" (Isaiah 55:8). Putting our giving into the proper perspective, and opening our hearts to receiving the blessings, even if it's just a smile on someone's face or a heartfelt "Thank you," purifies our intentions.

I attended a Men's Summit at Gateway Church in Southlake, Texas, and during this particular retreat, the testimony of one speaker shifted my perspective regarding expectations as a result of tithing and giving. Todd McIntyre, Gateway's Men's Pastor, related his experience of giving until it hurt, in the expectation that God would bless him financially because he had faithfully continued to give away his money, even when it didn't make sense. Todd's refrain to God was, "Okay, I did what You said, now it's Your turn." So he gave. And waited. Gave. And waited some more.

For two years Todd received seemingly nothing. He whined and complained, and then God finally spoke: "Your whining does not motivate me. I'm not your Mama. I'm your Daddy. If you want to live, you have to have faith." God continued: "Your motives are wrong. You gave for the wrong reason. Your foundation is on sand. You need to put it on Rock." Pastor Todd's lesson was not only in faith and right motives, but in perseverance and surrender. "When I finally gave up," Todd said, "my life started turning around."

In the book of Acts, chapter 20, the Apostle Paul concluded his farewell address to the presbyters of the church at Ephesus with words that have almost become a cliché: "... keep in mind the words of the Lord Jesus who himself said, 'It is more blessed to give than to receive'" (Acts 20:35b). The reference is from the Book of

Ben Sira: "Do not let your hand be open to receive, / but clenched when it is time to give" (Ben Sira 4:31 NABRE). The blessing is in the giving itself, the joy that enters your heart when your hand is released.

Mary's giving heart always amazes me; my wife truly gives to bless others, and she lives out her Spiritual gift of giving as naturally as Hannah lives out her gift of goofiness. Mary serves to serve, to meet a need, to satisfy a want. One evening she chatted on the phone with one of her best friends, Kacy Lanier Brown, and during the conversation Kacy admitted to going through a rough patch financially as her husband, Justin, labored hard to build up his business. She'd been applying for financial assistance to bridge the gap, but had run into obstacle after obstacle during the application process. Later that week Mary asked me what I planned to tithe the upcoming Sunday. "$96," I said. "Why?"

"I want to buy a grocery store gift card and give it to their family," she declared. I agreed, and that Saturday we met Kacy at a local craft fair and wine festival where she sat under a canopy selling rustic picture frames, hat hangers, and flags her husband had fashioned from scraps of old wood, used horseshoes, and corrugated steel. She'd been there all day, through rain, wind, and sparse crowds, and had sold just enough to pay the vendor fee and clear a little bit more to take home.

When we arrived, one last heavy downpour had already rumbled through the area, and the early evening sun shone brightly in the crisp blue sky. As we helped Kacy break down the canopy and pack away her wares, Mary called her aside and presented the gift card to her. Kacy looked at her, tears welling up in her eyes. "No," she said. But my wife insisted.

"Look at me," Mary told her. "Listen to me. Every week my husband and I tithe and we've been blessed for it." She pressed the card into Kacy's hand. "This is our tithe for this week. You are our church, and this is what church is about, it's about taking care of each other." Kacy took the card and both women cried. And Mary's joy – and Kacy's! – was complete.

Both the Old and the New Testaments contain many stories about people enthusiastically giving, and the subsequent results of this encouragement, service, and material sacrifice. In 1 Chronicles 29, King David announced to the Hebrews that not only had he stored up the materials to construct the Temple, he had also donated his personal fortune of gold and silver "because of the delight I take in the house of my God" (1 Chronicles 29:3a NABRE). He then asked the people, "who else will contribute generously and consecrate themselves this day to the LORD?" (v 5b). The Hebrews "came forward willingly and contributed for the service of the house of God..." (v 6b-7a). And what they contributed blew away David's personal sacrifice in spades. Because of David's enthusiasm and his heart for God, "the people rejoiced over these free-will offerings, for they had been contributed to the LORD wholeheartedly. King David also

rejoiced greatly" (v 9). As a result of these blessings, God in turn blessed the Hebrews, through
Solomon, with a "princely house" where God
dwelled among His people (2 Chronicles 6:2a
NABRE).

Later, after Joash became king, he commanded that the tax "for the tent of the
testimony" (2 Chronicles 24:6b NABRE) be collected to repair the Temple his own grand-
mother had damaged. "All the princes and the
people rejoiced," (v 10a) and contributed so much
to the cause that the money chest had to be
emptied several times, and "they restored the
house of God according to its original form, and
reinforced it" (v 13b). The people gave with joy,
and as a result they were again blessed with a
Temple befitting the King of the universe.

In the book of Acts, Luke recorded that in
the early church in Jerusalem, "all who believed
were together and had all things in common;
they would sell their property and possessions
and divide them among all according to each
one's need. They ate their meals with exultation
and sincerity of heart, praising God and enjoying
favor with all the people" (Acts 2:44-45, 46b-47a
NABRE). The result? "And every day the Lord
added to their number those who were being
saved" (v 47).

In Philippians chapter 4, the Apostle Paul
praised the church in Philippi for materially
supporting his needs despite their severe poverty
and affliction. In fact, Paul told them they were
the only church to do so. Consequently, he was
more excited about the Philippians' spiritual

"profit that accrues to your account" (Philippians 4:17b NABRE) rather than the contribution itself; God looks more favorably at the attitude of the giver rather than at the gift itself.

In 2 Corinthians 8b (NABRE), Paul used the example of the Philippian church's continued eager insistence on giving out of "their joy and their profound poverty" to support the church in Jerusalem as a rally call to the church in Corinth to follow through on their own commitment. In 2 Corinthians 9:6-7 (NABRE), Paul wrote, "Consider this: whoever sows sparingly will also reap sparingly, and whoever sows bountifully will also reap bountifully. Each must do as already determined, without sadness or compulsion, for God loves a cheerful giver." I was fascinated to learn that the word "cheerful" in verse 7 is the Greek word "hilaros," which means "hilarious."[36] We should all put on our Groucho Marx glasses and strive to become hilarious givers!

So... are you a hilarious giver, giving not out of compulsion or fear but with sacrificial willingness and expectancy? Are you eager in your giving? Does giving put a smile on your face, or does the thought of it make your hands sweat? Are you following the example of the widow who dropped her last two coins into the temple offering box out of pure, unencumbered hope (Mark 12:41-44)? Or are you more like the Pharisee who fasted and tithed and exalted himself before men and God while praying in the temple (Luke 18:10-14)? As Jesus said, that kind of attitude produces its own reward.

Have you ever thought that when you give, God may repay you with gifts even more priceless than money? Like opportunities? Good health? A ten-year-old car that keeps running flawlessly? What about experiences, or revelations of heaven on earth? A good marriage? Godly children? Divine appointments? Or talents beyond the realm of human possibility? God does give good gifts, we just need to open our hearts and eyes to what He is already doing, what He is already giving to us, and be thankful: "In all circumstances give thanks, for this is the will of God for you in Christ Jesus" (1 Thessalonians 5:18 NABRE).

"God is able to make every grace abundant for you," the Apostle Paul assured the church in Corinth, "so that in all things, always having all you need, you may have an abundance for every good work" (2 Corinthians 9:8 NABRE). We have the assurance that, as Paul himself experienced, "the one who supplies seed to the sower and bread for food will supply and multiply your seed and increase the harvest of your righteousness" (2 Corinthians 9:10 NABRE). In other words, don't worry about what you give, because God will abundantly provide for your needs. After all, He is YHWH Yireh, the God Who provides; it's all His anyway!

CHAPTER 13

JOY IN OBEDIENCE

Blessed are all who fear the LORD,
who walk in obedience to him.
— Psalm 128:1

My obedience to what I know to be right brings
me joy. My disobedience to what I know is right
brings me misery.
— Matthew Kelly, *A Call to*
Joy: Living in the Presence of
God[37]

Hannah jumped out of her booster seat, folded her arms, and stomped to her bedroom. "This just hasn't been a good day!" she yelled. *Slam!* The door smashing into the doorframe shook the house. Mary looked at me. I shrugged and shook my head. We both took another gulp of wine and continued eating dinner in silence. Welcome to dinnertime at the Hughes house, where getting our six-year-old to leave the nutritionally-barren desert of meat, cheese, and Ranch dressing and venture into the verdant garden of rice, potatoes, and anything colored green is like getting our dogs to quit barking at jackrabbits: it's been challenging.

For the most part, our household is a sanctuary of fun, learning, and family time, but when disobedience sails in on the winds of Hannah's blooming personality, peace jumps overboard. Some call it being "strong-willed." Mary and I call it "pour me another glass of wine." First came the flat-out "No," followed by copious applications of timeout. However, as the petals of Hannah's personality continue to unfold, the ubiquitous "Why?" has replaced "No." Now acknowledgement of our imperatives results in one of three responses: "Yes," deliberate ignoring, or nuclear meltdown.

"What did we do?" Mary asked as we finished dinner to the accompaniment of muffled crying coming from Hannah's bedroom.

"Nothing," I replied. "I blame Eve." And, indeed, isn't that where all this disobedience stuff started? You have to admit, Adam and Eve had it pretty good at the beginning. They walked with God, talked with God, hung out with God, and tended the Garden of Eden for God. Shoot, they even ran around naked without having to worry about the police showing up! God provided for all their needs and He asked only one thing from them in return: to keep their hands off the fruit of the tree of the knowledge of good and evil. This was the first application of the well-known parental utterance, "Don't touch the hot stove."

God desired worship, relationship, and obedience, and He lavished on Adam and Eve pleasure and every good thing. And what did our ancestral parents do? Eve caved in to a talking serpent. Just like we still do today. Why? Because we want to be in control. Some things never change.

When God speaks, He expects His people to obey, and the primary source of His commands and His will for us is Scripture. "If God tells you to do something, do it!" I've heard many times. Like the old E.F. Hutton commercials, when God talks, people need to listen! Why? Because God doesn't just speak to hear Himself talk, like we sometimes do. No, when God tells us to do something, whether it's through His Word, other people, or directly through His Spirit, it's for our own good. When we obey God, we honor Him. When we act on His directives, commands, and precepts, we glorify Him.

This book is the result of obedience; God told me to write it, so I did. Despite the fact that I lived in ignorance of the true meaning of joy and its real and practical manifestation as a fruit of the Holy Spirit, I obeyed God's directive, stepped out in faith, and started researching and writing. Throughout this journey I've witnessed miracles resulting from obeying God's commands. Despite leaving a well-paying job with a relatively secure future, God the Provider has "somehow" maintained my family's financial well-being, leaving little doubt He's managing all aspects of my new career. Despite my initial ignorance about joy, God has directed me to books, blogs, websites, and other folks living joy day-to-day, revealing bit-by-bit the potential of existing in a state of permanent joy despite circumstances. Don't get me wrong, living a life of obedience to the Father sometimes isn't easy – that darned old flesh still seems to get in the way – but I move forward knowing it's what I'm being called to do. Indeed, it's what we're all being called to do.

Throughout the Old Testament God is clear about the results of obeying His commands: things will go well. "Walk in obedience to all I command you, that it may go well with you," God said through His prophet Jeremiah (Jeremiah 7:23b). Here Jeremiah was reminding the Hebrews of God's promises in Leviticus 26 in return for their obedience. In the Book of Deuteronomy, Moses wrote: "So be careful to do what the Lord your God has commanded you; do not turn aside to the right or to the left. Walk in obedience to all that the LORD your God has commanded you, so that you may live and prosper and prolong your days in the land that you will possess" (Deuteronomy 5:32-33).

Several years ago one of our church small group members described an epiphany he experienced while driving. "If you stay within the speed limit," God told him, "you remain under my covering of protection. But if you speed, you move out from under that covering." Speed limits have been imposed in an effort to protect folks from the consequences of irresponsible driving; God's precepts have been given to protect folks from the consequences of sin. Remain obedient and things will indeed go well for you.

When Hannah disobeys us then asks why we've disciplined her, Mary and I sometimes paraphrase what the Apostle Paul wrote to the church in Ephesus, regarding the Fifth Commandment: "Children, obey your parents in the Lord, for this is right. 'Honor your father and mother' – which is the first commandment with a promise – 'so that it may go well with you and that you may enjoy long life on the earth'" (Ephesians 6:1-3). The alternative, we tell her, is for us to eat her. A little hyperbole never hurt anyone, but it sometimes leads Hannah to paraphrase back to me Paul's next line: "Fathers, do not exasperate your children" (Ephesians 6:4a). Smart aleck.

Obedience to God's commands also leads to power. In Deuteronomy 11, Moses instructed the Hebrews, "If you carefully observe all these commands I am giving you to follow – to love the LORD your God, to walk in obedience to him and to hold fast to him – then the LORD will drive out all these nations before you, and you will dispossess nations larger and stronger than you" (Deuteronomy 11:22-23). And in Deuteronomy 28:1, God promised to raise Israel "high above all the nations of the earth" as long as they heeded His voice and obeyed His commands. In Deuteronomy 28:9, Moses reiterated this truth: "The LORD will establish you as his holy people, as he promised you on oath, if you keep the commands of the LORD your God and walk in obedience to him."

As we keep God's commands as grace-covered children of the New Covenant, as we yield ourselves to God's authority, as we love Him and fear Him, we open our hearts and our lives to receive His unlimited power for His Kingdom, His glory, and our joy. Indeed, Jesus told his apostles before His arrest, "Very truly I tell you, whoever believes in me will do the works I have been doing, and they will do even greater things than these, because I am going to the Father. And I will do whatever you ask in my name, so that the Father may be glorified in the Son. You may ask me for anything in my name, and I will do it" (John 14:12-14). And later He promised the disciples, "Ask and you will receive, and your joy will be complete" (John 16:24b).

Obedience to God's commands also results in prosperity. "Walk in obedience to him, and keep his decrees and commands, his laws and regulations, as written in the Law of Moses," David told his son, Solomon, before he died. "Do this so that you may prosper in all you do and wherever you go" (1 Kings 2:3). In the Second Book of Chronicles, the Chronicler described Hezekiah, one of the most upright kings of Judah, as a man who "did what was right in the eyes of the Lord" (2 Chronicles 29:2). And as a consequence of "doing what was good and right and faithful before the Lord his God," Hezekiah flourished. "In everything that he undertook in the service of God's temple and in obedience to the law and the commands, he sought his God and worked wholeheartedly. And so he prospered" (2 Chronicles 31:21).

Obedience to God's commands leads to long life. After Solomon asked God for wisdom instead of long life and wealth, God told him, "If you walk in obedience to me and keep my decrees and commands as David your father did, I will give you a long life" (1 Kings 3:14). And again, the Fifth Commandment says, "Honor your father and your mother, as the Lord your God has commanded you, so that you may live long and that it may go well with you in the land the LORD your God is giving you" (Deuteronomy 5:16). Whenever Hannah questions the wisdom of what we're asking her to do, Mary and I remind her that obedience leads to things continuing to go well for her, even though what we'd like to say to her is Bill Cosby's famous line, "You know, I brought you in this world, and I can take you out."[38]

Obedience to God's commands also keeps you planted firmly in God's presence, and this brings about a joy that cannot be taken away. "'If you do whatever I command you and walk in obedience to me and do what is right in my eyes by obeying my decrees and commands, as David my servant did,'" God promised Jeroboam through the prophet Ahijah, "'I will be with you. I will build you a dynasty as enduring as the one I built for David and will give Israel to you'" (1 Kings 11:38).

Disobedience to what we know to be right, on the other hand, has consequences of its own, and for the Hebrews of the Old Testament, it got ugly. God cast Adam and Eve out of the Garden of Eden after they ate the forbidden fruit. God turned Lot's wife into a pillar of salt after the angels specifically commanded Lot and his family not to look back at the destruction of Sodom and Gomorrah. God stripped away all but one of Solomon's kingdoms after his fall from God's favor. God allowed the Israelites to be captured and taken into exile to Assyria and to Babylonia. In both Leviticus 26 and Deuteronomy 28, God very clearly defined the consequences of disobeying the Law. The Israelites, for their part, very clearly defined the term "stiff-necked people."

But it's from the single act of obedience by a young Hebrew virgin girl named Mary that forever changed history and brought permanent joy into the world:

> *In the sixth month of Elizabeth's pregnancy, God sent the angel Gabriel to Nazareth, a town in Galilee, to a virgin pledged to be married to a man named Joseph, a descendant of David. The virgin's name was Mary. The angel went to her and said, "Greetings, you who are highly favored! The Lord is with you."*
>
> *Mary was greatly troubled at his words and wondered what kind of greeting this might be. But the angel said to her, "Do not be afraid, Mary; you have found favor with God. You will conceive and give birth to a son, and you are to call him Jesus. He will be great and will be called the Son of the Most High. The Lord God will give him the throne of his father David, and he will reign over Jacob's descendants forever; his kingdom will never end."*
>
> *"How will this be," Mary asked the angel, "since I am a virgin?"*

> *The angel answered, "The Holy Spirit will*
> *come on you, and the power of the Most High*
> *will overshadow you. So the holy one to be born*
> *will be called the Son of God. Even Elizabeth*
> *your relative is going to have a child in her old*
> *age, and she who was said to be unable to*
> *conceive is in her sixth month. For no word*
> *from God will ever fail."*
>
> *"I am the Lord's servant," Mary answered.*
> *"May your word to me be fulfilled." Then the*
> *angel left her.*
> *– Luke 1:26-38*

"May your word to me be fulfilled." Christian obedience to God's commands under post-resurrection Grace is just as relevant as Hebrew obedience to God's commands while living under the pre-resurrection Law. Just as the moral spirit of the Law remains as fully alive today as it did 5,000 years ago, obedience to Jesus' new command to love one another encompasses "all the Law and the Prophets," as Jesus responded when tested by the expert in the law in Matthew 22:40.

"If you love me, keep my commands," Jesus told his apostles before his arrest (John 14:15). And as Adam and Eve's disobedience in the Garden led to the Fall, Christ's obedience to the cross led to humankind's reconciliation with God. "Son though he was," the author of Hebrews wrote, "he learned obedience from what he suffered and, once made perfect, he became the source of eternal salvation for all who obey him and was designated by God to be high priest in the order of Melchizedek... For the joy set before him he endured the cross, scorning its shame, and sat down at the right hand of the throne of God" (Hebrews 5:8-10, 12:2b).

From the obedience of a humble Jewish girl to the obedience of her Son, mankind has been reconciled with the Father. "And being found in appearance as a man," Paul wrote in his letter to the church in Philippi, "[Jesus] humbled himself by becoming obedient to death – even death on a cross!" (Philippians 2:8). By Christ's example, and by our willingness to step out in faith and become obedient to our calling to live as children of God under the New Covenant, we are made righteous. By grace we have been freed, and it is by love that we are called to remain obedient to the God who loves us so much "that he gave his one and only Son, that whoever believes in him shall not perish but have eternal life" (John 3:16).

"There is an indescribable joy that comes from being obedient," Caroline Barnett wrote in *Willing to Walk on Water*. "When all is said and done, you have willingly been part of a greater cause."[39] Now if I could only get Hannah to listen to me when I tell her to pick up her clothes and turn them right-side out, all would be truly right with the world.

CHAPTER 14

JOY IN EVERYDAY MIRACLES

I will give thanks to you, LORD, with all my
*   heart;*
I will tell of all your wonderful deeds.
I will be glad and rejoice in you;
I will sing the praises of your name, O Most
*   High.*

$-$ Psalm 9:1-2

After finishing a six-hour-long editing session one afternoon, the writing urge pawed at me, turned circles at my feet, looked up at me with its imploring brown eyes, and whined. "Okay, okay," I sighed. I scratched its ears and it cocked its head and wagged its tail tentatively. It had been days since I'd written anything other than criticism of someone else's writing; it was time to play catch with my muse. But I had a problem: while I'd spent the past few days editing and catching up on housework, fear had slipped in and was now perched on my monitor overlooking my keyboard. It sneered at me.

I've been at this writing game off and on for over thirty years, and I'm here to tell you that even after so many stories, articles, chapters, poems, and books, the fear of failure still haunts the dark recesses of my brain. Luckily, God's Spirit is alive and well and dwelling in my heart! Over the past several years I've learned how to wield the power of Truth against this fear, but even though it is emaciated, weak, and a crust of its former self, it can still bite. So that afternoon, as I cast off the editor's hat and slipped on the writer's beanie (you know, the one with the little propeller on top), I struggled with doubts, a writer's worst enemy.

I knew what I wanted to write. I even had an outline tucked away in my head, but as my fingers touched the keyboard in creative rather than editorial mode, a feeling of dread, heaviness, and foreboding swept over me. The fear of failure continued to hover over my keyboard, and its ugly sneer deepened into a snarl of impending triumph. Saliva dripped onto my number pad. But I took a deep breath and typed nonetheless. What came out seemed forced, contrived, amateurish.

I knew I could do far better, but as I tried to gain creative momentum, fear settled back on its haunches, stuck a toothpick in its lips, and guffawed. Yes, it *guffawed!* But I kept pushing until... something shifted. Words began to line up in an orderly fashion, giving shape and form and grace to the thoughts, stirring them to action. Ideas gelled, paragraphs rose up, points declared themselves. But the fear of failure remained firmly seated on top of my monitor. Granted, the sneer had reversed into a frown on its misshapen face, but it hadn't budged. It leered, staring at my fingers and the words forming on the screen.

Then the most wonderful thing happened. The piece I worked on was called "A Change in Perspective," and the intention of the essay was to convey how changing the way we look at a situation can shift not only the outcome of the situation, but also the moment-by-moment experience of that situation. We all have the ability to reframe our experiences, no matter what they are. As such, life is a matter of perspective; we always have a choice about whether or not to believe the thoughts flying through our heads, and how we subsequently act on those thoughts. "We take captive every thought to make it obedient to Christ," the Apostle Paul advised in 2 Corinthians 10:5.

I had wanted to include in the essay the Scripture from Isaiah that says something like, "My thoughts are not your thoughts and my ways are not your ways," but didn't know the citation off the top of my head. While writing the piece, I'd included Jesus' teaching about prayer: "your kingdom come, your will be done, on earth as it is in heaven" (Matthew 6:10) and had to look up that reference as well. I jumped onto the internet and brought up Bible Gateway's web page, and the Verse of the Day contained the following Scripture:

"For my thoughts are not your thoughts,
neither are your ways my ways,"
declares the LORD.
"As the heavens are higher than the earth,
so are my ways higher than your ways
and my thoughts than your thoughts."
— Isaiah 55:8-9

I laughed. And laughed. And cried and laughed some more. "Thank you, Daddy," I sobbed. "Thank You, thank You, thank You." I'd just received another kiss on the cheek from a God Who cares about me more than I'll ever know, and Who *loves* to encourage His children with little, strategically-placed miracles just like that. Defeated yet again, the fear of failure slid off my monitor and slinked away to its dark cave to lick its wounds, and for the rest of the day I happily played catch with my muse. I finished the essay the next morning covered in joy, peace, and a sense of triumph. I posted it on my blog page three days later.

Throughout the Bible, God makes it clear that as we press into Him, study His precepts, and obey His commands, He will increasingly open our eyes and our ears to the mysteries of His Kingdom. On this earth, there's more than meets the eye; God's Kingdom is literally at hand. In the Second Book of Kings, chapter 6, the king of Aram, enraged because the king of Israel always knew where he'd set up camp, deter-mined to expose the mole within his ranks. "'Tell me! Which of us is on the side of the king of

Israel?'" the king of Aram demanded of his officers.

"'None of us, my lord the king,' said one of his officers, 'but Elisha, the prophet who is in Israel, tells the king of Israel the very words you speak in your bedroom'" (2 Kings 6:11b-12). The king of Aram set out to capture Elisha, and as the Arameans surrounded the city of Dothan, where the prophet resided, Elisha's servant panicked:

> *"Oh no, my lord! What shall we do?" the servant asked.*
> *"Don't be afraid," the prophet answered. "Those who are with us are more than those who are with them."*
> *And Elisha prayed, "Open his eyes, LORD, so that he may see." Then the LORD opened the servant's eyes, and he looked and saw the hills full of horses and chariots of fire all around Elisha.*
> — 2 Kings 6:15b-17

Elisha asked God to open his servant's spiritual eyes and give him a glimpse into the reality that surrounds us. The Bible doesn't explicitly indicate the servant's reaction to what he saw, but I'm sure it was the same reaction we have when God kisses us on the cheek with one of His countless everyday miracles: joy, relief, encouragement, and confidence. I bet that guy wore an ear-to-ear smile for days and weeks after his encounter with the heavenlies. Maybe he wore it for the rest of his life!

In all three of the Synoptic Gospels, Jesus concluded several parables with the phrase, "Whoever has ears [to hear], let them hear" (Matthew 11:15, 13:9, 13:43; Mark 4:9; Luke 8:8, 14:35). And in the Book of Revelation, Chapter 2, Jesus said, "Whoever has ears, let them hear what the Spirit says to the churches" (Revelation 2:7, 11, 17, and 29). As the Spirit opens our spiritual eyes to see beyond the natural, He likewise opens our spiritual ears to listen to, comprehend, and witness the reality of the supernatural, the Kingdom of God on earth, where miracles are an every-moment occurrence.

Miracles happen all the time; I know – I've witnessed countless, both large and small, and I've heard stories from others that can only be caveated as miracles. Why does God still dole out miracles? For our joy and encouragement, and for His glory. As a daddy myself, there's nothing like hearing the squeal of surprise and unfettered joy erupting from my daughter as she opens up a gift she's been nagging us about. At six years old, Hannah's at the age where nothing's subtle, especially when asking for something she wants. She doesn't drop hints, she just asks, asks again, asks yet again, asks continuously, like the persistent widow in Luke 18, until we either yell "no," sigh "yes," or begin plotting for the delivery of the gift wrapped in surprise. Hmm, sounds a little like God when *we* pray, eh?

As Mary prepared for Hannah's sixth birthday party, we asked her what she wanted. "I want a magic kit!" she told us. And during the weeks leading up to the party her desire never wavered, so we passed that information on to Grandma and Grandpa, who set out to fulfill the mission. Mary had hired a professional magician to entertain Hannah and the dozen little girls at the party, so after the magic show ended, the cake and ice cream were consumed, and the piñata was smashed to confetti, we herded the sugared-up girls back into the living room so Hannah could open her gifts.

After Hannah had torn off the wrapping paper from a few boxes, Grandma handed her a long package. I pointed the video camera at her and stood in anticipation of the incipient culmination of weeks of expectancy. Hannah began peeling off the paper, and the instant she realized what she held in her lap, she squealed with joy. I mean, *squealed! That* is why God still performs miracles! *That* is why Daddy still hands out fish instead of snakes, and eggs instead of scorpions. He's a good Daddy, and He loves it – loves it! – when we not only recognize His miracles with joy, but when we make known His marvelous deeds to the world. Like Hannah, the more we squeal about our magic, the more we glorify the gift Giver.

Like I said, I've witnessed countless miracles, many small, some extraordinarily large, and it's funny: I seem to remember the small miracles more than I do the large ones, maybe because they seem to happen so often now. These are little signs He's intimately involved in my moment-by-moment existence, that He cares about me more than I'll ever realize.

In the fall of 2012 Mary and I (well... Mary) decided to replace the worn out, stained carpeting in our living room and hallway with laminate flooring. We're do-it-yourselfers, so we ended up in the flooring department at Lowes poring over various types and styles of laminate, asking for advice, and comparing colors. Both of us quickly arrived at the same color and style: Pergo Hand Scraped Heritage Hickory. Independently deciding on the same style and color at the same time could be considered a miracle in itself! On that day, all the various colors in the Pergo style we wanted sold for $2.99 per square foot. When we got home that afternoon, I calculated how much it would cost to cover our entire living room and hallway. The laminate, vapor barrier, trim boards, and the flooring itself exceeded our $1,350 budget. We'd planned to install the flooring over Christmas break, but put off buying the material until we came up with a more affordable alternative.

A day or two later a Lowes flyer arrived in the mailbox. I opened it and casually flipped the pages to see if there was anything we couldn't live without. As I turned to the flooring page, I noticed the ad featured Pergo laminate for the original $2.99 per square foot. Then I saw it: Pergo Hand Scraped Heritage Hickory, *$2.49* per square foot, the only style that had been discounted. *What the – ?!* I quickly calculated the new cost to redo our living room and hallway: $1,350, give or take! We rushed to Lowes, secured a whole pallet at the sale price, and got to work. Three days later (which was another miracle in itself!) we hosted Christmas at our house featuring a brand-new living room floor. Oh, and you know what's even cooler? Both of the saws I used to cut the wood – the table saw and the compound miter saw – had been given to us by generous neighbors. For free. Yet *another* miracle! Praise God and pass the vapor barrier!

God reveals Himself every moment of every day, and He loves it when we not only recognize Him in the everyday miracles, but when we squeal with delight when we open the package and recognize the gift as coming from Him. And what's even better? When we store up those stories of God's awesomeness in our hearts and then tell those stories to the world. "Declare his glory among the nations," urged the psalmist in Psalm 96:3, "his marvelous deeds among all peoples." God gets the glory and we get the pleasure and the joy. As the psalmist sang in Psalm 107:21-22:

> *Let them give thanks to the LORD for his*
> *unfailing love*
> *and his wonderful deeds for mankind.*
> *Let them sacrifice thank offerings*
> *and tell of his works with songs of joy.*

Be blessed, keep your eyes and ears open for those miracles, and tell of His works with songs of joy!

CHAPTER 15

JOY IN A PERSON

One of the most easily identifiable characteristics of Christian happiness is attractiveness... Christian happiness... is tremendously attractive and very contagious.
  — Matthew Kelly, *A Call to Joy: Living in the Presence of God*[40]

"Dad, you're weird," Hannah declared one morning as I waited for the toaster to eject my English muffin.

I grinned. "Why do you say I'm weird?" I asked, sipping my coffee.

"Because you're a writer."

Yes, I am a writer, but first and foremost I'm a child of God walking to the beat of a heavenly drum. For years I stifled my bongos under a blanket of conformity, smiling nonetheless, because, as the eyes are the windows to the soul, a smile is the window that opens to hope. And now that the blanket has been stripped off, my drum beats loud and strong as I walk the path marked out for me through the jungle of status quo.

Mother Teresa once said, "Let us always meet each other with a smile, for the smile is the beginning of love."[41] A smile can change your demeanor in an instant if you take the time to consider the possibilities painted in the brightness of the offering. As I walk through life, I pray my smile touches people's lives in some small way, with some small hope, with some small encouragement.

"Anyone who has a continuous smile on his face conceals a toughness that is almost frightening," said Greta Garbo.[42] In so many ways, I wear this smile as a badge of defiance against an enemy who'd like nothing better than to steal it away and replace it with a scowl of defeat.

The Bible is filled with examples of people whose lives brought joy to others. In the book of Esther, King Xerxes, king of Persia and Media, honored Mordecai, Queen Esther's cousin, because Mordecai exposed a plot to kill him. And because Esther revealed she was, in fact, a Jew, destined to be annihilated under the "vile" Haman's orders, King Xerxes ordered Haman impaled, elevated Mordecai to second in command, and gave Mordecai authority to write a decree allowing the Jews to avenge themselves against their enemies.

Because the edict authorized God's people to stand their ground, they ended up killing over 75,000 of their enemy. Mordecai then established the celebration of Purim "as the time when the

Jews got relief from their enemies, and as the month when their sorrow was turned into joy and their mourning into a day of celebration" (Esther 9:22).

In his gospel, Luke recounts the angel Gabriel's announcement of John the Baptist's birth and ministry to Zechariah, John's father. "He will be a joy and delight to you," Gabriel told the old priest, "and many will rejoice because of his birth, for he will be great in the sight of the Lord. He is never to take wine or other fermented drink, and he will be filled with the Holy Spirit even before he is born. He will bring back many of the people of Israel to the Lord their God. And he will go on before the Lord, in the spirit and power of Elijah, to turn the hearts of the parents to their children and the disobedient to the wisdom of the righteous – to make ready a people prepared for the Lord" (Luke 1:14-17).

John the Baptist became a joy and a delight to Zechariah, but more importantly, he became a joy and a delight to those who paid attention to his message, repented, and turned back to God. But why did Gabriel tell Zechariah to keep John away from wine or other fermented drink? Because, as the last prophet before Jesus' coming, God had filled him with the Holy Spirit in the womb, and God wanted to ensure folks didn't confuse John's intense joy for inebriation. He was drunk with the Holy Spirit! And he became a joy for others as he pointed his followers to the Messiah.

Earlier, I told the story of my friend, Jason Hoffman, and how a woman approached him at work and asked him, "What's the source of your joy?"

Jason pointed up and responded "It's all Him." Jason displays his joy in not only his beaming countenance and gentle character, but in his willingness to step out and serve others. He's a true model for what it means to be a joy-filled Christian walking in the footsteps of Jesus, our ultimate Joy. Another inspiring person I know who's wrapped in a mantle of gladness is Amy Copeland, Preschool and Special Needs Director at New River Fellowship.

Talk about someone who radiates joy! The woman displays it as brightly as the moon wears the sun's reflection. The moment she walks into a room dressed in her almost perpetual smile, you can't help but feel lighter and happier. "I think of joy as a deep feeling of happiness and contentment," Amy told me, "knowing that no matter what happens, I am going to be okay, because God has me in His hand and He is in control."

Amy knows all about God's control, and God's grace. While growing up, she aspired to become a teacher, and while still attending the University of Kentucky, she married her husband, Barry. After graduating, Barry's job led them to Cincinnati, then to Ridgeland, Mississippi, where she gave birth to their first daughter, Kaylyn. "I was passionate about my child as any new mom would be," she said, "but perhaps a little more so, since I never really knew if I would be able to have any children at all." Amy had been diagnosed with Polycystic Ovarian Syndrome, and her doctors had cautioned her that conceiving a child could be very difficult. "Once I saw that little girl wrapped up in that tiny little hospital blanket, I knew my role as a parent was going to be the biggest and most important role I would ever have here on earth. This new passion would spark everything I did during the next fifteen years."

As her oldest daughter went off to kindergarten, her second miracle baby, Ashton, missed her sister so much she begged her mom to go to school as well, even though she was only two. So Amy applied and got a teaching position at New River's Kids Day Out, or KDO, program, and Ashton attended KDO's three-year-old class. "I fell in love with the kids, and from those years of serving God's little ones, I learned I was supposed to work with young kids. I had found my Joy and my Calling." So over the next four years she studied for her Texas Teaching Certification and substitute taught at a local elementary school.

"During my last two years of subbing," Amy said, "I got a call to cover a class for a lady I knew, Angie, an aide in the Autism Unit. She told me she felt terrible that day and asked me to cover her on Thursday. I said hesitantly, 'Sure.' Until that moment, I had avoided the Special Education Department like the plague. I didn't feel comfortable in those classrooms at all, and I had no desire to work inside one."

"Well, little did I know what God was about to do," she continued. "I worked for Angie on Thursday and received a call from her again that evening. She asked if I could work for her again on Friday. I thought, *Well, I survived one day, I guess two won't hurt.* Her last words to me during our phone conversation on Thursday evening were, 'Thank you, Amy. By the way, the class is going on a field trip and you can wear my T-shirt that is in my locker. I just don't think I'm going to beat this illness before the weekend.' Wow! One day in the Autism Unit and now I was headed to the Special Olympics at the Weatherford High School football field. God is funny! He just *loved* putting me outside of my comfort zone. I realized that day that special needs kids are just like any other kid. They need to be loved, nurtured, corrected, and just have fun playing."

Tragically, the Sunday after Amy took the kids to the Special Olympics, Angie passed away from the swine flu. The school asked Amy to continue to substitute teach until they found someone to take over the position permanently. She stayed on for two and a half more months, but Amy never applied for the position; she'd given in to the voice in her head that she didn't have what it took to tackle the job long term. The lead teacher later told her she should have applied for the position.

"I never thought of myself as a Special Education teacher until the moment she told me she wanted me to stay. That's when I became the 'Sped Sub.'" She then substituted at the Autism Unit almost daily, and at the encouragement of the lead teacher, Amy went back to school and obtained her Special Education Certification. "I love teaching and I love kids, *all* kids! God has had me on quite a journey to show me what my passions and abilities truly are, and working within my passion in a way that brings glory to Him. This brings me *joy!*" Amy understands it, and she demonstrates that joy amazingly well.

Another person who understands joy is Kayla McMillan, also known as Kayla Mac. Just being around this enthusiastic young lady for a few minutes can lift up your mood, and, like Amy, Kayla also had an epiphany that painted her life with permanent joy. It started in her freshman year of high school when she failed her standardized state assessment tests – all of them. Then her best friend died. "I think my ninth grade year was my turning point," said Kayla, "I saw my best friend the night before, then I found out the next day she was dead in a car accident."

In addition to struggling with the heart-breaking loss of her best friend, Kayla also wrestled with feeling secure in her own identity. But the reality and finality of her best friend's death opened her eyes to the fact that she was her own person. The tragedy spurred her to question what she was going to make of herself. "So I determined Kayla Mac was gonna be me. I was scared nobody would recognize me," she said.

"Throughout high school I made a name for myself," she explained. She really wanted to become an athlete, but "I wasn't good at sports. I tried basketball and I tried volleyball." She even did track, but "God had a different plan: I became an athletic trainer. I got to stand on the field. I got to be at every game. I did athletic training for football, then I did basketball. I wouldn't change anything, I was so excited. The best years of my life were spent on the field."

"Fast-forward a couple of years," continued Kayla, "and this is where my joy *really* started. For several years I was in depression and nobody knew it. I had my first boyfriend and he cheated on me and it was one of those 'Oh my gosh, nobody's gonna like me now' moments. After him, it just kind of crumbled, and I asked 'God, do You even care about me?' I remember several times asking Him, 'Why am I here? I'm on this planet to do nothing. What am I supposed to do right now? I don't care about anything, I have no hope.' There was no hope for me."

But the Lord soon answered her questions very dramatically. One day, as she drove to school, she saw a spider on the windshield of her truck. "I used my windshield wipers to get it off and it flew to the driver's side. I rolled down the window, grabbed a water bottle, and hit it, and as I hit it I swerved. I was looking down for some reason, when all of a sudden I heard 'Look up!' And I thought, *Okay, it's just me in the car,* but He goes, 'Look up, look up, *look up!*' and I looked up, but it was too late. I hit the guardrail, broke it completely off." She had crossed onto a bridge the moment she swerved, and as she punched through the guardrail, missing both a tree and a sign, she threw her arm across her face and thought, *This is it. This is it. This is where I die. I'm coming to see Jesus. This is it.* "I flipped and I ended up upside down. I opened my eyes – it felt like hours later – but I opened my eyes right after and I thought, *What's going on right now?*

and there was smoke everywhere." She realized that, miraculously, she was okay. She grabbed her phone and crawled out through the driver's side window, now collapsed to half its original height from the six-foot drop.

A neighbor had heard the crash and called 9-1-1 as he hustled to the scene. When he arrived he asked Kayla if she was okay, and as the reality of the moment came rushing in, she started crying. The man advised her to call her parents, and on the fifth try her dad answered. Because she was so distraught, Kayla handed the phone to the neighbor, who explained what had happened. He told him to meet her at the hospital.

Soon the ambulance arrived. "I was sitting on the edge of the bridge where the guardrail was gone," Kayla said, "and looking at all my stuff spread out everywhere. I was all muddy and blood was everywhere, and they walked up to me and said 'What are you doing?' and I said, 'What do you mean?' and he said 'You should not be there – you should be in *there*.'" The emergency worker pointed at the mangled truck lying upside down in the creek bed. At that instant her neck started hurting, so they put her in a neck brace, loaded her into the ambulance, and rushed her to the hospital.

"They got all the monitors hooked up and they took X-rays, and I found out I had no broken bones, no kidney damage – everything was intact. Everything." The neck pain, she learned later, had been caused by the stress of the situation; she had been hunching her shoulders to the point of pain. And the doctors told her that if she hadn't flung her arm across her face as she plunged off the bridge, she would've ended up with a mangled face because of the flying glass.

"I had a bruise and it went away the next day. I hit my knee against the wheel and my hip against the dashboard, so I had a little bit of tenderness, but no scar. I went home and I was just kind of lying there and I heard God clearly say, 'Do you see it now? You're not done. There's a reason why you're here. I have more for you. I could've taken you, but I decided not to because I have more for you.' I said, 'Okay,' and from then on I knew this was my turnaround. That was the climax. I need to live every day like He's called me to, and I said, 'I'm not gonna be depressed anymore, there's a reason why I'm here, and I'm gonna go do what He's called me to.'"

Since then she's shed her depression, clothed herself in God's mercy, and allowed Him to transform her into a living, breathing expression of the fruit of the Holy Spirit. "I just want to give other people hope – don't give up on yourself," she said. "Don't let the enemy steal your joy. I know the end of the story, so why get defeated? He's been defeated, so why do we still let him defeat us?"

With folks like Jason, Amy, and Kayla, who so readily demonstrate what it means to live joy moment-by-moment, the answer to that question is: we don't have to. "You are the light of the world," Jesus said. "A town built on a hill cannot be hidden. Neither do people light a lamp and put it under a bowl. Instead they put it on its stand, and it gives light to everyone in the house.

In the same way, let your light shine before others, that they may see your good deeds and glorify your Father in heaven" (Matthew 5:14-16). Indeed, each of us is called to be a light for others to glorify God and to be examples of His grace, mercy, power, love. And joy.

CHAPTER 16

JOY IN SUFFERING

Joy emerges from the ashes of adversity through your trust and thankfulness.
— Sarah Young, *Jesus Calling*[43]

When Fred Chapman woke up on the morning of Saturday, August 8, 2009, he had no idea his world would soon be flipped upside down. A racetrack chaplain for the Central Motorcycle Road Racing Association since 2003, Fred looked forward to supporting and ministering to the racers at Hallett Motor Racing Circuit in Hallett, Oklahoma. His youngest son, Jake, then thirteen, was scheduled to compete in a mini endurance race at Hallett while his 19-year-old son, Zac, warmed up for the WERA Nationals at Virginia International Raceway in Danville, Virginia. Zac, already a professional racer, planned to do well enough that weekend to pay for tires, gas, and racing fees for the AMA Pro event at Virginia International the weekend after.

Zac had taken his own motorcycle onto the track that morning to log a few practice laps, but while rounding one of the turns something went wrong. He lost control of the powerful motorcycle. Instinctively he tried to correct the heavy bike's trajectory. "I started to fall and I saved it," said Zac, "but when I did, it sent me off the track at an angle you don't normally do. It usually doesn't happen that way." He hit the weathered, hard tire wall head on at 60 to 70 miles per hour. Zac and the motorcycle decelerated in an instant, sliding along the barrier in a crunch of metal, fiberglass, plastic, and flesh. He skittered to a stop in the grass, facedown.

By the time the corner workers reached him and turned him over, Zac insisted on getting up, but the officials wouldn't let him. After the track ambulance arrived, the crew transferred him to a backboard, strapped his head down, and transported him to the pit area where he talked to his team owner and insisted he was okay. However, when Zac removed his helmet he began complaining about severe neck pain. Another ambulance then drove him to the local hospital for a CT scan.

Soon after the crash, Fred received a phone call from Zac's team owner telling him what had happened. Because Zac had appeared relatively coherent and intact, Fred wasn't immediately alarmed. He hung up and continued to carry equipment to the staging area, helping his younger son's team set up for the upcoming four-hour endurance race.

"I soon got another call," said Fred. "It was the emergency room doctor – he was on his personal cell phone – and he said, 'Mr. Chapman, I've got your son. We're going to give him a CT scan because he's not answering all the questions right.'" Not responding correctly to the questions was a sign of a concussion. Fred hung up after asking the doctor to call him when he received the results.

"It wasn't ten minutes later my phone rang and it was that same number," Fred recalled. "My first thought was, 'Well, you can't get the results of a CT scan that quickly.' I answered the phone and the doctor said, 'Mr. Chapman, I'm sorry to inform you, but when we put Zac into the CT scanner and started the scan he went into a coma and aspirated.'" The medical crew performed an emergency tracheotomy, then flew him via helicopter to Roanoke Memorial Hospital Trauma Center in Roanoke, Virginia.

A friend rushed Fred to Tulsa International Airport, and three hours later he was on his way to Roanoke. On the flight to Virginia, the man sitting next to him offered to pray for him and Zac. Until that moment Fred hadn't invited the Holy Spirit into the situation, so as the man prayed over him, Fred also prayed: "Holy Spirit, all of my Christian life I've heard You say that You'll give us peace beyond understanding," he implored. "There's no way I could understand that right now, but I want that peace." Peace and relaxation suddenly flooded over him. Back pain he'd suffered from for twenty-seven years melted away, like he'd just received a full-body massage. "That's when I laid my head back in the seat and closed my eyes, and I started talking to the Holy Spirit. That's when I heard Him tell me, 'Don't worry about Zac, I'm going to fully restore him.'"

On that promise, Fred rallied for his son after doctors confirmed he'd suffered from massive trauma to both his frontal lobe and his brain stem. During the impact, Zac's brain had torn loose from his cranium, a condition known as "brain shear." For all intents and purposes, the impact destroyed his frontal lobe. The neurosurgeon at Roanoke Memorial urged Fred to let Zac go, but he confidently refused. Joy and peace settled over him. "When you hear from God it gives you a peace," Fred explained. "The key to that is getting quiet and having the communication between you and God through the Holy Spirit. When you hear from God, you have to be obedient to carry out what He says and do it."

Because of the swelling, surgeons removed Zac's cranium from above his eyebrows to the temples and across the top of his head, and for nearly three months he lay in a coma on a respirator. Fred never gave up hope in God's promise, and he never left Zac's side. After Zac was flown back to Fort Worth, a medical crew transported him to Kindred Long-term Acute Care Hospital, where, five days later, the staff managed to remove Zac from the respirator. Three days after that, they succeeded in waking him from the coma, but he remained in a vegetative state. Four more weeks passed before he was transferred to Baylor Institute of Rehabilitation in Dallas. There doctors reattached the piece of bone removed from Zac's cranium to protect his brain from any further injuries.

After successfully completing this procedure, the neurosurgeon at Baylor confirmed the status of Zac's brain. "His frontal lobe is just like jelly lying in the bottom," he told Fred. "Lifeless, just destroyed." The area where his frontal lobe should have been was concave. Because reattachment of the cranial bone was intended for protection and nothing more, the doctor cautioned Fred not to expect any "big results" from the surgery.

"I understand," Fred replied.

After the surgery the medical team conducted CT scans every two hours throughout the night to monitor Zac's brain for swelling. "At six the next morning I was sleeping at Zac's feet in a chair, and the doctor came rushing into the room and startled me," Fred said. "He really freaked me out saying, 'Mr. Chapman! Wake up! Come here, you've got to see this! You've got to see this!' He grabbed my arm and I threw off the blanket and here we go!" The neurosurgeon hurried Fred to the nurses' station where a bank of large computer monitors stood, each displaying a CT scan. He pointed to the computer screens. "As I looked at each one," said Fred, "I saw that the frontal lobe had come back. And I said to the doctor, 'What are you telling me?' He said, 'The frontal lobe has come back!'"

Over the next four and a half years Zac has recovered not only his frontal lobe but also its associated functions such as personality, demeanor, language, decision-making skills, and character. A true miracle. And although he still spends a lot of time in a wheelchair, Zac can walk with the aid of a walker, and he gives his physical therapy team a robust workout with his determination to press forward toward God's promise of full restoration. He texts on his phone, he writes, he reads, he talks, and he drives his Polaris 4x4 Razor ATV through the woods. And more than anything he continues to inspire people with his positive attitude, his sense of humor, and his continuing recovery.

"People are always telling me," said Fred, "'You've been a great father, blah, blah, blah,' and I'm like, 'Dude, the only thing I've done is try to be obedient to God when He speaks.' But I don't want you to get a misconception – there have been tough times along the way. It's kind of that deal about joy coming in the morning, but, generally, the next day after the accident I was okay." Fred looked at his son, emotion welling up in his piercing blue eyes. "Zac's been my encouragement. What I see in him is the joy that he has, the great outlook on life, and everything else. He's so motivated. I'm around him every day, so I get more blessing because I see it, and that encourages me."

My life experience has not been as intense and challenging as Fred and Zac Chapman's, but even so, I've got my own scars from the top of my head to the bottom of my feet, literally. My body is a visual testament to not only my rough-and-tumble childhood, but also of a man fighting to define, discover, and ultimately live out his God-ordained destiny. Some scars I laugh about, like the slice across the crown of my scalp caused by my brother Ron clocking me over the top of the head with a toy hoe when I was five, or the mark on the bottom of my right heel where emergency room doctors had to cut out a toothpick I'd stepped on when I was eleven.

Some scars are evidence of a disconcerted past and my continuous warring against perfectionism and worry, like the five-inch gash from my sternum to my bellybutton, reminding me how a bleeding ulcer almost killed me – twice – before I turned 21. Other scars, both mental and physical, are permanent marks of past anger, shame, and extreme unsettledness, like the jagged tear on the inside of my right elbow, ripped open as I punched a plate-glass window in a fit of rage. There are psychological scars of a six-year struggle with clinical depression and spasmodic dysphonia. Even now these can become inflamed as the fear of slipping once again into that hell on earth tries to nudge its way back into my life. Thank God those scars have faded over the years; He has truly turned my mourning to gladness as He's anointed me with the oil of joy.

But what have I learned from all of these scars? I'm tired. But I'm also persistent. I ache, but for the most part, I'm now at peace. Though I don't feel like it at times, I'm also incredibly resilient; I don't give up. Ever. I'm humbled. And after fifty years, I've finally opened myself up to being used as a vessel for God. He disciplines me and He lets me go through some horrendous experiences to build me up, not to tear me down. Like a sword hardened in a blast furnace, I have been – and am still being – put through the fire to purge me from imperfection and sinfulness. I'm tough as carbon steel, a battle-hardened warrior for God.

One late summer afternoon Mary, Hannah, and I stopped at a local produce stand on our way into town. While Mary picked through the okra, I perused the other fresh offerings, like vine-ripened tomatoes and sweet-smelling canta-loupes. While selecting a cantaloupe to take home, I chatted up one of the farmers, a big man with a round, sunburned face and large hands. During our conversation I lamented the failure of my tomato crop that year. The farmer weighed in on my lack of tomato-growing luck. "Do you water them a lot?" he asked.

"Every day," I said proudly.

"That's too much," he declared. "Hold off watering them until they start to wilt. Let 'em stress and they'll produce."

Let 'em stress and they'll produce. Isn't that what God does with us? He allows us to go through temptation, to be tested, so that we produce abundant fruit for His glory and the glory of His Kingdom. "We have all had human fathers who disciplined us and we respected them for it," said the writer of the Book of Hebrews. "How much more should we submit to the Father of spirits and live! They disciplined us for a little while as they thought best; but God disciplines us for our good, in order that we may share in his holiness. No discipline seems pleasant at the time, but painful. Later on, however, it produces a harvest of righteousness and peace for those who have been trained by it" (Hebrews 12:9-11).

As Christ-followers we are not immune to trials. Jesus said so Himself: "In this world you will have trouble. But take heart! I have overcome the world" (John 16:33b). Not we "might" have trouble, not we "may" have trouble; no, we "will" have trouble. That's part of the hardening process, part of the raising up as warriors for the Kingdom. But when we do have trouble, our job is to endure, hope, and hold on to our joy as our Daddy transforms us from sinfulness to holiness, from flesh to glory. God's in the demolition and rebuilding business; He holds our hands as He turns ashes into beauty and weeping into dancing.

Jesus has already overcome the world, and in that truth we are urged to trust He knows what He's doing and to seek out the lessons He's revealing as we undergo trials, no matter how severe. All trials are life-changing, but it's up to us to put into perspective the direction, depth, and character of that change. As my wife put it, "Just because we've already won doesn't mean we won't have to fight the battles. It doesn't mean the devil isn't going to win sometimes!" But even when the devil wins, he still loses, because, in our case, a scoreless inning does not result in a lost game but a chance to review the film, adjust our strategy, and come back out swinging.

In his exhortation to the Jewish Christians, James encouraged the first-century followers of

Christ to hold on to their joy even as they faced various sufferings: "Consider it pure joy, my brothers and sisters, whenever you face trials of many kinds, because you know that the testing of your faith produces perseverance. Let perseverance finish its work so that you may be mature and complete, not lacking anything" (James 1:2-4). And what is our reward for this persistence? Heaven. "Blessed is the one who perseveres under trial because, having stood the test, that person will receive the crown of life that the Lord has promised to those who love him" (James 1:12).

Jesus suffered, and we followers of Christ would be arrogant to think we could be immune to suffering. Nowhere in the Bible does God promise life on earth would be easy. Or fair. Or painless. "But he was pierced for our transgressions, /" wrote the prophet Isaiah, "he was crushed for our iniquities; / the punishment that brought us peace was on him, / and by his wounds we are healed" (Isaiah 53:5). The point: Jesus suffered a horrible torture and death, yet His death restored our relationship with God and allowed us to approach the Throne of Glory without shame. Jesus' suffering led to pure joy, for God and for us, and because He modeled suffering for us, we should not expect to be spared, even to death, because we can't even begin to fathom what Jesus went through.

Just look at the apostles: of the eleven original apostles who remained faithful to Jesus, ten of them suffered horrific deaths as martyrs. The Apostle Paul spent a good portion of his ministry chained up, a prisoner for his bold proclamation of the gospel, before being put to death. And history flows with the blood of countless others who have sacrificed – and continue to sacrifice – their lives defending the Good News. God expects us to take up our own cross and follow Him, even into the throes of immense suffering, for His glory and for our perfection.

But is it really possible to get to a point in your life where, like Paul, you can experience joy while chained to a prison wall? Or to maintain joy while suffering persecution like the Thessalonian church and the other oppressed Christian communities he ministered to? Or, as tradition has it, to be as joyful as the Apostle James the Greater appeared to be when he faced beheading? He exuded so much confidence that a false witness who had testified against him became convinced of Jesus' true nature and was beheaded along with the apostle with the same sword.[44]

"You can still experience joy through suffering because of what God heals you *from*," explained Renee Crenshaw, Women's Pastor at New River Fellowship. Like many folks, I'd struggled to wrap my arms around James' exhortation in his epistle to consider it pure joy whenever we suffer. How could the pain, the depression, the rage, the overwhelming darkness of what I'd been through in the past be considered "pure joy?" To me it was pure hell. I couldn't relate. But Renee shined the light of truth on my exasperation: we can look back on the things of the past from which we've been delivered and experience joy *now*. We can take what was created for evil and, with God's grace and guidance, flip it upside down and use it for the benefit of the Kingdom. Like Jesus' death on the cross, joy, as Renee explained, "changes our perspective on what happened to us."

When she was a little girl her parents turned a deaf ear to the fights between her siblings. "My brothers had knock-down drag-outs where the big kid was always beating on the little kid. It was a Sunday tradition," she said. The family would arrive home from church and her brothers would start fighting. "I thought it was normal, that the biggest brother got to beat up the little brother, with the kids screaming for mercy." Because of this experience, Renee made a vow that her own children would never treat each other that way. "And they don't. Our kids usually don't speak ill of each other. They just don't fight. So what the enemy tried to make for evil has turned out completely different. Of course, we didn't do it perfectly, but I still think we can experience joy after the fact. He takes the ashes and turns them into beauty."

As Renee related, my life has also been one of both joy and suffering, but along the way I've come to realize the only way to learn the really big lessons in life – the epiphanies – is to go through hell and emerge on the other side, not unscathed, but wiser. One of the most effective ways to grow is to face suffering head on, not avoid it. We need to suffer. We need to fail. Mary and I both tell Hannah there's nothing wrong with failure, that failure is part of learning. If I was successful at everything I did, would I ever learn? No, I'd be bloated with pride, a lesson for others in how *not* to live life. Worse, would I ever learn dependence on God?

In America, we're raised to be independent – it's our national hegemony, our motto, our pride, our mission statement; we worship the self-made man, we idolize independence. Our programming tells us asking for help is a sign of weakness, especially for men – just look at all the jokes about men not stopping and asking for directions. What does that ever get us except a disgruntled wife and a car running on fumes out in the middle of nowhere! But life is all about suffering, and that suffering ultimately leads to joy, pure joy, joy unfettered, the fruit of the Holy Spirit. Why? Because God is our Comforter, and our suffering and our weakness allows His full Glory to be manifested through our trials.

I love the Apostle Paul's confession in his Second Letter to the Corinthians regarding his thorn. "In order to keep me from becoming conceited," Paul confessed, "I was given a thorn in my flesh, a messenger of Satan, to torment me. Three times I pleaded with the Lord to take it away from me. But he said to me, 'My grace is sufficient for you, for my power is made perfect in weakness'" (2 Corinthians 12:7b-9a). Paul never elaborated about what his thorn actually was, but whether it was a speech impediment, an adversary, or bone spurs in his feet, he pressed on in his mission to preach the gospel despite his affliction. *Despite* the thorn, Paul persevered. *Despite* the thorn, Paul became one of the most influential early Christian leaders in church history. *Despite* the thorn, he prevailed because God's power triumphed over Satan's attempt to extinguish the fire of the Spirit in Paul's heart. As I mentioned at the beginning of this book, joy is *despite*...

This anecdote about Paul is one of my favorites because I can relate to it so well. When suffering with depression and spasmodic dysphonia after my first wife left me, I prayed for God to take away the physical and mental manifestation of the evil pervading my life, especially because it seriously affected my job, my pursuit of writing, and my personal life. But in the throes of my suffering, in the pit of depression, in the rage, the whining, the wall pounding, I continued to clench an idol I didn't realize had so much power over me: pride. It wasn't until God purged out that sin, as He did Job's, that my heart was opened to the deeper healing He intended for me throughout the entire experience.

When I finally released pride and gave in to Daddy's discipline, compassion, and comfort, I began to heal spiritually, mentally, and physically. For six years I relied on His grace and His sufficiency, and at the end of those six years He released me, seemingly overnight, from my thorn, my messenger of Satan. "It is amazing how full Scripture is of comfort for mourners," C.H. Spurgeon preached, "because the Lord's objective is that the mourner be comforted."[45] Even though most of the time I didn't realize it, God held my hand throughout that entire ordeal,

He pressed my head against His bosom, He sang songs to me and held me tight. He comforted me.

It's funny, I'm an engineer by education, a man well-versed in mathematics, from simple arithmetic to calculus and differential equations. Even though I struggled with it during high school, I comprehend math, I understand numbers, I "get" mathematical concepts given enough time. I've lived in the world of mathematics the vast majority of my half-century existence, but it wasn't until I was 49 years old and home-schooling my daughter when I learned that math is the study of patterns. Doh! No one had ever explained it to me that way before. And here it was, laid out in plain English in a first grade homeschool curriculum! It was a true epiphany – if a teacher had explained that to me back in say, oh, first grade, I may have done even better at it.

And with that revelation I put two and two together and arrived at this: our experience of life is much like mathematics. God has laid out before us a challenge called life here on earth. From the beginning – even before the beginning – He graciously planted in our hearts a specific pattern to which we're drawn: His will, our dream. He desires for us to live out that dream from the start, but the antagonists – other people, our pride and selfishness, Satan, the world at large – get in the way. And so we suffer. But God doesn't give up on us. In fact, He allows us to go through those challenges to discipline us, teach us, hone us, and toughen us up. As the Apostle Paul assured in his letter to the Romans, "And we know that in all things God works for the good of those who love him, who have been called according to his purpose" (Romans 8:28).

So for those of you who are mathematically inclined, here's a little equation I came up with to explain the meaning of life:

$$\sum_{time=0}^{\infty} Suffering(time) = JOY!$$

For those who don't give a whit about math, it all comes down to this: when put into the proper frame of reference, the sum of all of our suffering over the timespan of life here on earth equates to joy. Factorial!

When I asked Zac Chapman what keeps him going, his response was inspiring: "I believe that God has, as Dad said, fully restored me, so I look forward to that day and I work toward it. But I want to be sure I'm happy where I'm at, not just looking forward to that day, but that I'm content where I am. And being content in doing that gives me hope, being happy where I am now."

And that's something we can all count on.

CHAPTER 17
JOY IN NATURE

God writes the gospel not in the Bible alone, but on trees and flowers and clouds and stars.
— Author unknown, commonly attributed to Martin Luther[46]

The whole earth is filled with awe at your
wonders;
where morning dawns, where evening fades,
you call forth songs of joy.
— Psalm 65:8

If you're questioning God's existence, or whether or not God is still actively involved in day-to-day reality... open your eyes! If you're struggling with life, with daily problems, with suffering, anger, depression, wondering where God is... look around! He surrounds us! If you're wondering whether or not God still speaks directly to His people, whether or not He still performs miracles, or if He's still in charge at all... take a walk in the woods!

Italian actress Eleonora Duse proclaimed, "If the sight of the blue skies fills you with joy, if a blade of grass springing up in the fields has power to move you, if the simple things of nature have a message that you understand, rejoice, for your soul is alive..."[47] Yes, rejoice! As King David sang in Psalm 22, God lives in the praises of His people, and as composer Alan Hoyhaness said: "I've always regarded nature as the clothing of God."[48] Take a minute, step outside, and see what God is wearing today.

The most joyful memories of my childhood are of walks in the forests of New York State. There the pines and maples and sumacs wrap their branches around everyday life. Houses are built like nesting boxes within the trees, and they gradually succumb to nature's blanket as moss grows on everything not exposed to direct sunlight. Burdocks reach out and grab your wool leggings while you're hunting rabbits. Spring air erupts with the earthy aroma of turned fields, an atmosphere mixed with the sometimes nause-atingly-sweet smell of cow manure spread on the freshly-plowed dirt. The hazy air of mid-summer drips with the tangy scent of newly-cut hay, and the strong mushroom odor of rotting leaves kicks up under your boots as you scout for deer in the twilight of early fall. And always the walks...

The house I grew up in was planted on the edge of a several-hundred acre meadow rising up to a line of trees. Beyond this tree line spread another group of fields cultivated with feed corn and hay. And past those fields grew the woods, a deciduous hardwood forest packed densely along one of the parallel shale ridges carved out by glaciers during the last ice age. It was there one of my first memories of walking in the woods with my dad was formed, solidly hewn into my life's experience. To this day, almost a half century later, I can vividly recall parts of that walk in sharp detail.

The memory begins with Dad leading my two brothers and me into the woods through a dark opening in the corner of a hay field. I couldn't have been much older than eight or nine, and I remember it was late fall or winter because we wore heavy coats, mittens, and clunky rubber boots, and the trees towered above us bare-branched, black, and wet. Gray clouds pressed down and penetrated our layers of clothing with a wetness so thick we couldn't tell where sweat ended and the humidity began. The overgrown log road penetrated the woods, slick with mois-ture, the carpet of brown and gold leaves glossy, the ancient tractor ruts half-filled with black water and choked with reedy saplings reaching toward the canopy for any remnant of sunshine they could grab. That particular day they were grossly disappointed.

We tromped along the path immersed in wonder, three ducklings following our papa duck. He was clad in red-and-black checkered wool and brown canvas, topped with his fluorescent orange hunting cap, ear flaps raised up and chin strap unsnapped. We didn't say much. I remember wondering how long it took for saplings to sprout up, take root, and grow in the middle of the road. I remember the quiet strength of our daddy leading the way, the comfort in knowing that as long as we stuck by him we'd never get lost. We never did: he always knew the way.

After an hour or so we sat down on slimy, moss-covered logs and Dad opened up a brown paper sack and passed out our sandwiches, followed by the small, football-shaped plums Mom liked to pack in our school lunches. For some reason those plums, deep bluish-purple with a powdery white patina on the skin, stick out in my mind as a highlight of that walk. I'm sure we planted the pits when we were done, thinking one day we'd come back to discover four plum trees stretched out over our impromptu picnic spot.

After lunch we headed back to our warm house and four cups of steaming hot tea with milk and sugar waiting for us on the kitchen table. I can imagine the musky scent of the wilderness clinging to our clothes and wet boots and contributing one more layer to the senses as we testified to a winter's day well-spent outside with our daddy, enjoying God's creation.

Joy still cradles me as I remember that day in all its details, a joy which helped germinate my love of walking in the woods, a joy borne of time spent with my dad and my siblings, of sharing wordless communion with each other and with nature. Since then I've spent countless days in the forest, from chasing cows escaped from their pasture to riding dirt bikes through the woods on uncut trails to walking through an unfamiliar tree line on a snow-covered day, alone with my thoughts and worries and prayers about college and hopes and dreams for my future.

Whenever I needed alone time I'd hit the woods, trails or no trails, walking with God clothed in His vestments of nature. I never got lost. Conversely, God always found me. For years this is how I found joy, reconciliation, the voice of God. And as I grew older and the busyness of everyday life took over, I yearned to rediscover that catharsis, that rejuvenation, that rebirth of hope and comfort and praise. Then one day I found it again, during a walk in the woods with my daughter.

Excitement hugged me as I dressed Hannah for a late January hike in the woods of North Texas. Since Mary was hosting a Perfectly Posh party for her best friend, Kacy, that day, I suggested taking Hannah on a walk at the Fort Worth Nature Center so we wouldn't be underfoot. Mary wholeheartedly agreed.

"Where are we going, Dad?" Hannah asked as we climbed into the car. "When will we be there? What will we see? How long will we stay?" She chattered like a squirrel discovering a freshly-dropped cache of pecans.

The day turned out to be cool and sunny, one of those crisp mornings overflowing with the brightness of a cloudless sky enhancing the sharpness of the tans, grays, olive drabs, and black-greens inked across the early winter landscape. My heart sang in anticipation of being able to introduce my own child to the joys of hiking in the woods, and as we drove through live-oak-strewn pasture land, past 20-acre ranchettes, and meticulously-coiffed neighborhoods peppered with two-story brick McMansions, I glanced back at Hannah's glowing face in the rearview mirror. And choked up. Joy overwhelmed me. Happiness coaxed tears into my eyes. I sniffled and smiled and knew without a doubt God rode along in the car with us, anticipating the walk as much as we did. It had been a long time – too long – since I'd been in the woods, and we missed each other intensely.

When we arrived at the Nature Center, we stopped at the Interpretive Center where Hannah attended an animal print-casting class with one of the docents. After Hannah poured plaster into her raccoon track mold, the docent gave us our own private track-spotting lesson in nature's classroom adjacent to the building while the castings dried. Hannah followed along, her eyes glued to the ground in search of tracks in the mud and dirt on the trail. She spotted coyote tracks, raccoon tracks, and even armadillo tracks. We messed with a fire ant mound, looked at the remnants of a controlled burn, and breathed in the quietness of God's grace.

After the guided hike finished, the docent left us on the far end of a field of native prairie grass, next to a line of trees. We found a bench, opened our lunch boxes, and ate our peanut butter sandwiches, apples, and snack bars in reflective silence. Flavors exploded on my palette as the fresh air heightened the sensitivity of my taste buds. I relished the moment as I remembered eating lunch in the woods with my dad.

Joy, peace, contentment, even a hint of melancholy mingled with the soughing of the crisp brown oak leaves and the waving prairie grasses. God sat with Hannah and me as resurrected memories mixed together with the creation of new memories.

We hiked back to the Interpretive Center, collected Hannah's track castings, and spent the rest of the day exploring the boardwalk, watching white-faced ducks from a bird blind, climbing on giant limestone boulders lining the Trinity River, and driving through the thick canopy of live oaks tangled with poison ivy and mustang grape vines. Hannah never complained, even when she tripped and fell face-first onto the slats of the boardwalk.

If God dwells in the praises of His people, He shows off His creative glory in the fabric of nature. The earth sings God's praises with the majestic uplift of snowcapped mountains, the raucous voices of migrating Canadian geese, the dancing of bluebonnets waving their blue and white hands to the One Who flung them across lush Texas fields. "The grasslands of the wilderness overflow; / the hills are clothed with gladness, /" wrote King David, "The meadows are covered with flocks / and the valleys are mantled with grain; / they shout for joy and sing" (Psalm 65:12-13).

Nature shouts for joy and sings in the explosion of Indian paintbrushes, black-eyed Susans, and white daisies blanketing a spring meadow. Nature shouts for joy and sings in the quietness of a copse blanketed in heavy wet snow, punctuated only with the slow drip of melting icicles and the chirp of a foraging titmouse. Nature shouts for joy and sings in the crash of waves on a shell-strewn beach, or in the growl of a thunderstorm building to the southwest in the absolute stillness of a late-spring afternoon.

In March of 2006, Mary and I drove to Las Vegas from Fort Worth for our honeymoon. On our way we headed into the aftermath of a blizzard that had swept across Arizona and New Mexico. For the first time in my life I witnessed the beauty of the snow-covered desert. We saw the transformation of aridness into the breathtaking irony of a desert snowscape, a juxtaposition of experiences that induced me to utter "wow" every few miles. We drove through drifts forming and reforming across Interstate 40 between Grants, New Mexico and Flagstaff, Arizona as the icy north wind plunged the desert into something more akin to the east shore of Lake Ontario than the lava fields of central New Mexico. We witnessed snow flurries falling from swollen purple clouds east of Las Vegas. But the most sublime manifestation of the beauty and power of God's nature was standing on the edge of the Grand Canyon's south rim with snow on the ground.

As I edged my way to the steel rail and peered over the precipice, my first look at the sheer grandeur of the Canyon took my breath away. But what it did to Mary was elevate her into a spiritual moment that left her crying, praying, and breathing in the glory of God. At that moment, as she drew in the truth of God's creative magnificence, her spirit met His Spirit at a zenith of pure joy that lasted the rest of the trip, and even to this day. "Nature is the art of God," wrote Thomas Browne in *Religio Medici.*[49] And God, through that art, elevated both of us to an appreciation of His absolute sovereignty and His desire to bring pleasure to His children through His creation. That moment was not only a kiss on the cheek from our Daddy, but an intense embrace, a hitching, sobbing, blubbering moment of pure rejoicing.

"I went to the woods because I wished to live deliberately," wrote Henry David Thoreau in *Walden*, "to front only the essential facts of life, and see if I could not learn what it had to teach, and not, when I came to die, discover that I had not lived."[50] To go to the woods, to sit quietly beneath the trees and reflect on God's beauty, or to walk on a blanket of newly-fallen leaves and breathe in God's glory, reconnects the soul to the heart of God's creativity, abundance, and exquisite order. To go to the woods rekindles the earthy relationship of man to the mud into which God breathed His Spirit. To go to the woods is to experience God's presence in the intricacies of a spider web sprayed with dew and glowing with the golden rays of dawn's first breath. To go to the woods is to embrace God's joy in the raw nakedness of His being, the ancient stirrings of the Garden, the interdependency of His creation. I go to the woods to see not only what it has to teach, but to pull out my lunch sack and feast on the presence of God.

Let the heavens rejoice, let the earth be glad;
let the sea resound, and all that is in it.
Let the fields be jubilant, and everything in
them;
let all the trees of the forest sing for joy.
Let all creation rejoice before the LORD, for he
comes,
he comes to judge the earth.
He will judge the world in righteousness
and the peoples in his faithfulness.
— Psalm 96:11-13

If you're questioning God's existence, or whether or not God is still actively involved in your day-to-day reality... open your eyes! His nature surrounds us with the real evidence of His desire to reveal His glory and to please His children. Take God's hand, step into the woods, and rejoice!

CHAPTER 18

JOY IN LETTING GO (AND LETTING GOD)

Jesus replied, "No one who puts a hand to the plow and looks back is fit for service in the kingdom of God."
— Luke 9:62

Our happiness and our surrender to God in all things are linked, but surrender is slow, painful, and often a struggle.
— Matthew Kelly, *A Call to Joy: Living in the Presence of God*[51]

My name is David C. Hughes, and I'm a budget junkie. For over thirty years I've been addicted to my budget. Not an only-on-weekends addiction, but a binge-every-night obsession. I'm sure most folks would rather shoot their eye out with a Daisy Red Ryder BB gun than put together a budget, but until recently I rolled around in it like a chicken in a dust patch! I'd literally redo my budget twice a day, depending on which direction and how strong the financial winds were blowing. Just ask my wife. For a season Mary took the reins of our family's day-to-day finances to help me reset my attitude toward money and God's ownership of it.

One evening she sat down at the computer desk to balance the checkbook. She added, subtracted, crossed out, verified, and re-verified the bank's ledger against what the checkbook indicated. She added again, subtracted again, verified again, and finally arrived at an earth-shattering conclusion: "The checkbook's off by $700," she announced reluctantly.

I gasped. "In our favor, right?" My hands began to sweat, my face flushed.

"No, in their favor."

This can't be happening! I grabbed the checkbook and proceeded to re-do the math with exaggerated flourishes, hard-set jaw, and overly-loud mouse clicks. But it was happening. No matter how I turned the checkbook over and over, the numbers showed we'd made enough math errors to require us to pencil in a $700 loss. Granted, I'm not a person who gets angry with other folks very quickly, but money for me could be a hair trigger that sets off a volley of emotional firepower. I have to admit I let reaction override reason in that situation, and the brunt of my wrath rained down on my poor wife who was only trying to serve her anal-retentive husband and balance the darn checkbook.

It took several hours for me to finally let go of the mistake and forgive myself and my wife, but that episode also revealed to me the death grip I held on money, and how desperately I needed to loosen my clutch. It wasn't until I began to trust God, I mean *really* trust God, and embrace His Word and His promises of abundance, protection, and sovereignty that I could finally release the embrace I had on the spirit of Mammon and allow God to control my family's assets.

And when I let go, something miraculous happened: little-by-little, peace settled in and began to surround my thoughts about money. My control-freak micromanagement of finances relaxed a bit. I only did the budget once a week rather than twice a day. My need to know my net worth to the penny tapered off, then shriveled up and blew away. Putting my finances into God's hands led to a more confident obedience to His request to write this book and the myriad other books, stories, and essays He's planted in my heart to write. And bit-by-bit joy snuck in behind peace, slowly revealing itself in the fruits of obedience and trust.

One Wednesday evening at our church life group, during the call for praise reports and prayer requests, the subject of tithing came up. "I asked God for a better job and more money," confessed Charles Kincaid to the group. "And God answered my prayers with the job I now have. But I've lived without for so long I'm having a hard time taking that last step and tithing." Charles asked for prayers, but he inadvertently initiated a spirited discussion on the benefits and blessings of giving a tenth of your gross income to the church, per Old Testament tradition.

After fifteen minutes of joyfully bombarding Charles with enthusiastic and sometimes emotional testimonies of the very real results about giving out of the heart, one of our other members, Gilbert Banda, spoke up: "If God keeps the birds fat," he said. "Then why wouldn't He take care of us like that?" We all nodded in agreement.

Gilbert had alluded to one of my favorite passages in the Bible, Matthew 6:26: "Look at the birds of the air; they do not sow or reap or store away in barns, and yet your heavenly Father feeds them. Are you not much more valuable than they?" And Psalm 37:25 says, "I was young and now I am old, / yet I have never seen the righteous forsaken / or their children begging bread." I can testify personally to this truth: in a half century of life on this earth, I've never been without. Oh, I'd be lying if I told you I hadn't experienced lean times, but I've never been forced to skip a meal because food wasn't available to eat. I've never been forced to go out in the cold in short sleeves because a coat wasn't available to wear. I've never had to sleep in the elements because shelter wasn't available to cover me. The Lord has *never* left me nor forsaken me. When I let go of finances by actively sacrificing with tithes and offerings, I let God bless me with abundance. But more importantly, He has blessed me with amazing stories, both mine and those of others, so numerous they'll fill up another book. When I finally let go of my dearth mentality and started giving abundantly, confidence walked in with peace and joy and made itself right at home in my heart.

In 1990 I married my first wife. I was 26 years old and she was 21. Pride marched right down the aisle with us, as did fear and lust. Greed also sauntered along for the ride, and selfishness did its part to point us away from each other and the relationship. After a three year slow burn, my first wife left me with an empty house, a broken heart, and a worthless gold wedding band. Joy had left the building. Despair set up shop and depression swept me into the dark world of hopelessness. For three years I tried to function within a framework of normalcy; I went to work, got involved in divorce recovery ministry, continued to go to church. I also pressed on with writing and attending my read-and-critique group. But as I tried to hang on to my perception of normalcy, the depression turned clinical and snuffed out all but the last ember of hope as a disease called spasmodic dysphonia stole away my voice.

I drove home from work one evening after a particularly stressful bout dealing with the hitching, lurching, painful symptoms of the disease strangling me. People told me I sounded like a three-pack-a-day smoker. I stuttered. Vowel sounds stuck in my larynx. The spasmodic dysphonia had progressed to the point I began to avoid speaking. When I got home that night I barely made it to the bathroom before the gusher hit. I sat down on the tub step, pressed my hands against my temples, and cried. I cursed myself. I cursed God. I asked Him, "Why?" I asked Him when it would all be over. I kicked a shoe through a window pane. I turned like Peter at the Temple, denying God's very existence. I told Him quite assuredly that I'd lost all faith in Him, in relationships, in mankind, in myself.

When the faucets under my eyes trickled off, I shuffled out of the bathroom like a defeated old man, hunched and wasted and numb. "Sleep," I whispered to myself. "Sleep." On the way to the couch I picked up my Bible and lay down on the sofa, cradling the book against my chest. I fell into a sleep haunted by nothing but a deep blackness...

"593."

I woke up. My sweaty fingers stuck to the Bible's cover. *God?* I didn't want to open my mouth, didn't want to speak. *Show me the way. Guide me to a passage in the Good Book that will bring me peace.* He reiterated: *593.* My mind jumped to "Old Testament, first column." Then "601" popped into my head. I opened my Bible, a book I had very rarely read, a book guarding its Wisdom until this moment. I turned to page 593 and began to read...

And now my life ebbs away from me,
days of affliction have taken hold of me.
At night he pierces my bones,
my sinews have no rest.

Yet should not a hand be held out

to help a wretched person in distress?
Did I not weep for the hardships of others;
was not my soul grieved for the poor?
Yet when I looked for good, evil came;
when I expected light, darkness came.
My inward parts seethe and will not be stilled;
days of affliction have overtaken me.
I go about in gloom, without the sun;
I rise in the assembly and cry for help.
I have become a brother to jackals,
a companion to ostriches.
My blackened skin falls away from me;
my very frame is scorched by the heat.
My lyre is tuned to mourning,
and my reed pipe to sounds of weeping.
                              — Job 30:16-17, 24-31 (NABRE)

"My God," I said out loud. I quickly finished the page and flipped to 601:

Would you refuse to acknowledge my right?
Would you condemn me that you may be
justified?
Have you an arm like that of God,
or can you thunder with a voice like his?
Adorn yourself with grandeur and majesty,
and clothe yourself with glory and splendor.
Let loose the fury of your wrath;
look at everyone who is proud and bring them
down.
Look at everyone who is proud, and humble
them.
Tear down the wicked in their place,
bury them in the dust together;

> *in the hidden world imprison them.*
> *Then will I too praise you,*
> *for your own right hand can save you.*
> — Job 40:8-14 (NABRE)

God spoke to me, held me in His arms, rocked me gently while I read the entire book of Job for the first time ever. Peace came over me like a blanket on a cold night. I shivered. I believed. For the first time as a Christian, I actually *believed*!

I believe now more than ever in God's infinite Mercy, unfathomable Love, ever-flowing Forgiveness. God smiled at me in that moment, and He's still smiling, has always smiled despite my denial of His very existence. "Would you refuse to acknowledge my right? / Would you condemn me that you may be justified?" (Job 40:8 NABRE).

I hung my head in reverence, repentance, and total surrender. Only an hour before I had cursed the Most High God in an attempt to create my own peace, to achieve my own justification. And despite my intense pride, He saved me. And as Job acknowledged God's greatness and omniscience, as he realized his pain and suffering were tests of his fidelity, I stood with him, shoulder to shoulder, and God blessed both of us. I began to let go of pride and selfishness that night, and I let God in for the first time in years. Maybe for the first time ever. Peace snuggled down with me. And perspective. Three years later the spasmodic dysphonia turned tail and finally left me alone. And it has not come back.

In Isaiah 43:18-19, the Lord spoke through the prophet, commanding, "'Forget the former things; / do not dwell on the past. / See, I am doing a new thing! / Now it springs up; do you not perceive it?'" Like the proverbial monkey reaching into the gourd, the Hebrews had grabbed hold of sinfulness and refused to let it go despite the elimination of Israel, the invasion of Judah, the capture of Jerusalem, and the Babylonian exile. God allowed His people to go through a long season of suffering, but He never gave up on them, never backed down on any of His promises. Through Isaiah's prophesies God promised restoration. But God implored them to let go of the past, to let go of sin, to let go of all the garbage and infidelity and idolatry. The exiled Hebrews had to let go and let God spring up a new thing. "I, even I, am he who blots out / your transgressions, for my own sake, /" said God in Isaiah 43:25, "and remembers your sins no more."

True to His promise, God held nothing against them; it was God's mercy, not the Hebrew's faithfulness, which set the people free. God extends that mercy, the gift of salvation, to all of His people, to this very moment. Let go and let God, and let joy return to its homeland: your heart.

CHAPTER 19

JOY STEALERS

"The thief comes only to steal and kill and destroy; I have come that they may have life, and have it to the full."
— John 10:10

Pastor Scott Crenshaw likes to say, "We talk about needing Jesus in the sweet bye and bye, when we die in the sky. But I need him in the nasty now and now!" Life isn't all fluffy pillows and soft puppies, Neil Diamond songs and winning lottery tickets. No, life in this fallen world can be grungy, dirty, complicated. Life can be boring. Life can be downright painful and wholesale depressing. Jesus Himself assured us life would be messy: "In this world you will have trouble," He promised. "But take heart! I have overcome the world" (John 16:33b). Sometimes life isn't a bowl of cherries but a manure pile ripening on a hot summer's day. "Be alert and of sober mind," the Apostle Peter warned. "Your enemy the devil prowls around like a roaring lion looking for someone to devour" (1 Peter 5:8). And prowl he does, doing what he does best: confusing us, stirring up trouble, establishing strongholds in our minds, attempting to separate us from the Word and the Truth. Stealing, killing, destroying. He devours our joy with relish like a six-year-old sucking down Oreo cookies dipped in a glass of milk.

When I first pondered this chapter, I jotted down a laundry list of things I considered joy stealers. The list included the idolatry of worldly security, the love of money, covetousness, busyness, distraction, people-pleasing, inflexibility, perfectionism, complaining, and worry. I had every intention of fleshing out each one of these negative attitudes, especially as they related to my life experiences. I'd even asked other folks what they considered to be joy stealers, and I received several thoughtful inputs. But the more I contemplated, the more I realized this: sin is the ultimate joy stealer. And what is sin but the deliberate agreement with the enemy of God to willfully engage in anything that goes against God's love.

"When I place anything in front of, or in place of, God," said Jason Hoffman, "it hinders my ability to see, hear, or feel Him. I believe that all the 'stuff' and 'patterns' of this world come from the enemy who wants to steal my joy. Satan is the only one, in my opinion, who can steal my joy, if I let him, which, after all, is his ultimate goal: to snatch each and every believer for himself, for us to worship him instead of the

Trinity. He accomplishes this when we begin to doubt God, or when we don't see His love for us, or can't see through our circumstances. Oftentimes all we see in front of us is our circumstances and how *big* they are instead of *how big* our God is!"

"Whoever dwells in the shelter of the Most High / will rest in the shadow of the Almighty, /" the psalmist wrote in Psalm 91. "I will say of the LORD, 'He is my refuge and my fortress, / my God, in whom I trust.' He will cover you with his feathers, / and under his wings you will find refuge; / his faithfulness will be your shield and rampart" (Psalm 91:1-2, 4). But when we move out from under His feathers for whatever reason, be it selfishness or pride, lust or fear, we distance ourselves from God's protection, and, like a good Daddy, He sometimes lets us learn the hard way why He told us not to touch the hot stove or to eat from the tree of the knowledge of good and evil in the first place. It's called free will, and sometimes the price of freedom is to be chained by it for a season.

By definition, being in God's presence means we are placed squarely within the realm of joy. According to Galatians 5:22, joy is second only to love in the list of the gifts of the Holy Spirit; being in God's presence (Love) results in the presence of Joy. As such, we give the devil our consent to steal our joy when we deliberately shift our heart out of the fullness of God's love and into the shadow of death. We hand our joy over to Satan on a silver platter then gripe when we realize he's accepted our handout. Oops. We have the power to willingly give our freedom over to the enemy, and all too often we're happy to exercise that freedom for all the wrong motives.

Quite literally we've been given an awesome choice with awesome consequences: choose life, and life will be ours; choose death and we'll receive it. We have the power to willingly give up our joy for the false belief that somehow griping and complaining can fix the evils of the world instead of proactively changing our minds and believing that what God says in His Word is true. We have the power to willingly cast off the security and the peace and the authority given to us by a God of infinite mercy and boundless love and wrap ourselves in the cloak of pride and impatience. "I know how to do it better. And faster!" we kid ourselves, then wonder why the wings fall off our dream before it even gets off the ground. A broken heart received from a smashed up dream can certainly be a killjoy.

Living for so many years in an environment heavily steeped in tradition, and profoundly skewed by an obsession with sinfulness, I never defined my existence within the realm of a loving and merciful Savior but within the context of a running list of sins I kept in my head. As a result, life for me became a living hell; joy could not stick around long in that poisonous atmosphere. I kept a meticulous record of wrongs, and this recordkeeping led to a pattern of obsessiveness, fear, and perfectionism that put me in the hospital three times and almost killed me once. I didn't live in love; I lived in terror of dying in a state of mortal sin. For me, life was slaving away day in and day out for my salvation. I pictured God as an angry deity out to get me, like that old Gary Larson *Farside* cartoon showing God sitting at His heavenly computer with His finger poised over the smite button. Ouch!

That wasn't life. That wasn't the experience of joy. In fact, that was the opposite of joy. That was hell, the absence of God by my own hand. What is joy but the continuous turning away from that which destroys and embracing that which brings life, and not only brings life, but brings life to the full? I want to embrace life to the full! I want to experience joy, not just moments of joy sprinkled over an ocean of misery and self-defeat, but real joy erected on the foundation of Truth and girded by the presence of God. How can we do that? We must gain control of our thoughts, acknowledging the Source of real joy, and using His Word to tear down the strongholds, battling the lies the enemy uses to diminish or destroy our effectiveness for the Kingdom of God.

Thwarting the devil and his schemes is a matter of recognizing his influence, and then changing our minds and guarding our hearts against these plans. The enemy is a master of twisted truth – just look at what he did to convince Adam and Eve it was okay to eat from the tree of the knowledge of good and evil. Just look at the temptations he threw at Jesus after His forty-day fast in the desert. Just look at what he did to influence the Sanhedrin to press for Jesus' death sentence. And just look at what he whispered to Pontius Pilate to convince him to go along with the wishes of an insecure Jewish leadership resolved to protect a tradition of power and control. But know this: we don't have to listen to him. We don't have to relinquish our joy to the one who is hell bent on diminishing our effectiveness for the glory of God. We can take back our joy because it's our choice to fight for it. That joy is ours!

James, the first century leader of the Jewish Christian community in Jerusalem, wrote, "Submit yourselves, then, to God. Resist the devil, and he will flee from you. Come near to God and he will come near to you. Wash your hands, you sinners, and purify your hearts, you double-minded. Humble yourselves before the Lord, and he will lift you up" (James 4:7-8,10). Likewise, the Apostle Peter wrote, "All of you, clothe yourselves with humility toward one another, because, 'God opposes the proud / but shows favor to the humble.' Humble yourselves, therefore, under God's mighty hand, that he may lift you up in due time. Cast all your anxiety on him because he cares for you" (1 Peter 5:5b-7). We need to give Him *all* of our cares, and He promises to lift us up in due time. Knowing He will rescue us from the pit of hell for His glory and for our benefit will ultimately bring joy to our heart, "for our light and momentary troubles are achieving for us an eternal glory that far outweighs them all" (2 Corinthians 4:17). But it's our choice.

"Therefore, since we are surrounded by such a great cloud of witnesses, let us throw off everything that hinders and the sin that so easily entangles," the author of the Letter to the Hebrews wrote. "And let us run with perseverance the race marked out for us, fixing our eyes on Jesus, the pioneer and perfecter of faith. For the joy set before him he endured the cross, scorning its shame, and sat down at the right hand of the throne of God. Consider him who endured such opposition from sinners, so that you will not grow weary and lose heart" (Hebrews 12:1-3). How do we impede the enemy? How do we recognize his schemes, push back against his plans, and reclaim our rightful victory against his influence? How do we plant our flag on the mountain of joy? We need to recognize where these lies are coming from, hold these thoughts up against the gold standard of God's Word, and swing the Sword of Truth to slay the lies and tear down the strongholds the enemy tries to build in our minds.

"We demolish arguments and every pretension that sets itself up against the knowledge of God," the Apostle Paul instructed the church in Corinth, "and we take captive every thought to make it obedient to Christ" (2 Corinthians 10:5). How do we take those thoughts captive? By deliberately comparing the veracity of the thought to the Word of God. "The weapons we fight with are not the weapons of the world. On the contrary, they have divine power to demolish strongholds" (2 Corinthians 10:4). And what is the weapon we hold that's powerful enough to destroy these lies? God's Word: "... take up the shield of faith, with which you can extinguish all the flaming arrows of the evil one," the Apostle Paul wrote in his letter to the Ephesians. "Take the helmet of salvation and the sword of the Spirit, which is the word of God" (Ephesians 6:16-17).

The Bible is a story about sin and its consequences. But it is so much more than that. It's a story about God's mercy and His desire to establish and nurture a relationship with each of us. It's the ultimate love story, and with love comes joy. Jesus' sacrifice, "for the joy set before him," reestablished that relationship between God and mankind by eradicating our sins once and for all and reconciling us to a God Who loves us more than we realize and more than we'll ever know. The joy of the Lord *is* our strength, and to fully embrace that joy, to fully receive that strength, we need to let go of the sin that so easily entangles us and enter the presence of God with thanksgiving and rejoicing. After all, it's our choice.

CHAPTER 20

THE JOY OF HEAVEN

... what if Earth
Be but a shadow of Heaven, and things therein
Each to other like, more than on earth is
*   thought?*[52]

— John Milton, *Paradise Lost*

God created us in His own image for joy and for relationship with Him and with each other. On earth we catch glimpses of this happiness, Milton's "shadow of Heaven," but our ultimate joy is to enter into full unity with God, the saints, and His other righteous beings in heaven, where we will see Him as He is, face-to-face. In heaven we, too, will have our being in the eternal presence of God, and we, too, will join in singing, "'Holy, holy, holy / is the Lord God Almighty,' / who was, and is, and is to come" (Revelation 4:8) as we gaze upon the glorious radiance of our Creator. We, too, will dwell in endless joy in the moment-by-moment presence of the triune God.

But I can relate to Bram Stoker, who wrote in his short story, "A Dream of Red Hands:" "Ordinary men, to whom all things are possible, don't often, if ever, think of Heaven. It is a name, and nothing more, and they are content to wait and let things be."[53] When I was a kid I don't remember talking much at all about heaven, but boy did we talk about the alternative a lot! We obsessed about hell, and until just a few years ago I was convinced I was one moral banana peel away from slipping into it. Thank God He opened my eyes to the reality of salvation, grace, and mercy, but for way too long my conscience burned with visions of hellfire and brimstone straight out of Dante's *Inferno*; I knew how to wail, or at least whine, but gnashing my teeth was something I needed to practice.

Many years ago I read an article about hell that scared the living daylights out of me. In spirit, this harsh, condemning essay took what Jesus said in Matthew 7:13 about the narrow gate leading to life and reduced it to the width of a toothpick while widening the road to destruction from horizon to horizon. I roiled in shame and disbelief as I imagined breathing in the sickening odor of my soul cooking in the flames of eternal damnation. As far as I recall, the author never mentioned Jesus' assurance in Mark chapter 10 and Matthew chapter 19 that, with God, all things are possible, including salvation and eternal life, not by works but by God's grace. I wondered if I could do anything to avoid being heave-hoed into the lake of fire along with the other goats. It wasn't until the Lord revealed the truth of His love and my sonship that the burden of hell I'd carried for so long lifted, and the reality of my final destination began to sink into my frightened soul. But what is heaven, anyway?

The recent plethora of books and movies about heaven has brought our ultimate destination into the forefront of cultural awareness. But this reawakening to the reality of both heaven and our bodily resurrection is a resurgence of something the ancients and the early Christians embraced as part of their common mindset. The sheer number of references to heaven, the heavenlies, and the spiritual realm in both the Old and the New Testaments bears witness to not only the reality of heaven's existence, but also the extent to which the Jews and Christians alike discussed and accepted it. Even the Jews believed that prophets like Elijah and forefathers like Abraham, Isaac, and Jacob had already made it there (see 2 Kings 2:11 and Matthew 8:11). Jesus Himself said as much when He told the disciples the parable of the rich man and Lazarus: "The time came when the beggar died and the angels carried him to Abraham's side," Jesus said. "The rich man also died and was buried. In Hades, where he was in torment, he looked up and saw Abraham far away, with Lazarus by his side" (Luke 16:22-23).

So why is our vision of heaven vague at best, and cartoonish at worst, a picture of angels sitting on clouds and plucking at harp strings? Why is the vision of hell burned into our collective consciousness, but the picture of heaven is ethereal, nebulous, ill-defined? Why should we expect to experience joy in anticipating our arrival there when we don't have the foggiest clue what to imagine? If heaven is our final destination, and since we'll be spending a very long time there (like *forever*), why do we have such a difficult time building up excitement and anticipation for our ultimate resting place? It's sort of like trying to get excited about an upcoming trip to an exotic destination without doing any prior research about the locale. If you're like me, instead of being thrilled about the approaching journey, you'd probably be nervous about what to expect. Ignorance, in this case, does not result in bliss, but in indifference at best, fear at worst. But heaven is home and, as Dorothy said in the *Wizard of Oz*, there's no place like it!

"And let us run with perseverance the race marked out for us," the author of the book of Hebrews wrote, "fixing our eyes on Jesus, the pioneer and perfecter of faith. *For the joy set before him* he endured the cross, scorning its shame, and sat down at the right hand of the throne of God" (Hebrews 12:1b-2, emphasis mine). Jesus faced the shame of the cross and looked through the imminent horror with joy. Why? Or more importantly, how? Because He clearly saw the result of what He was about to do: redeem mankind, reestablish God's relationship with His creation once and for all, and open the gates of Paradise to those He is thrilled to call His sons and daughters. And as Jesus approached the cross, as He endured pain and suffering most of us will never experience, He focused on His ultimate destination, where He would soon arrive and take His place at the right hand of the Father, and where He now has all authority in heaven and on earth. He is, indeed, our High Priest, our advocate, our intercessor, our friend.

The Bible, God's word and authority, provides a clear vision of both heaven and hell, so, to me, it's somewhat surprising we don't have a more concise and wonderful vision of our ultimate home. Heaven is God's holy dwelling, a place He created and from which He rules the universe. It is a location inhabited by angels, both those loyal to God and those who have fallen; even demons and Satan himself can approach God. And since His crucifixion and death, Paradise is also populated with His saints, such as the repentant thief crucified next to Him, and all who enter will become like God and will gaze upon Him in all His glory, face-to-face.

Angels, both God's servants and those who stand against Him, travel between earth and heaven, and heaven can, and does, open onto the earth. In the Second Book of Kings, the prophet Elisha prayed that his servant's spiritual eyes be opened to see the reality of all that surrounds us: "And Elisha prayed, 'Open his eyes, LORD, so that he may see.' Then the LORD opened the servant's eyes, and he looked and saw the hills full of horses and chariots of fire all around Elisha" (2 Kings 6:17).

We, as believers, have already secured citizenship in heaven, and we are being called back to heaven even now. When people are saved by their professions of faith, their spirits are lifted to heaven and are "seated... with him in the heavenly realms in Christ Jesus" (Ephesians 2:6). So, in essence, we have dual citizenship until the moment of our earthly death. "For to me, to live is Christ and to die is gain," wrote the Apostle Paul to the church in Philippi while imprisoned for the gospel. "If I am to go on living in the body, this will mean fruitful labor for me. Yet what shall I choose? I do not know! I am torn between the two: I desire to depart and be with Christ, which is better by far; but it is more necessary for you that I remain in the body" (Philippians 1:21-24). Paul desired to be released from his bondage through death, to be with Christ in heaven, but he also recognized that, while his own suffering would come to an end, in death he could not continue to minister to and grow the Philippian church. For him, both were a source of joy.

In heaven both hope and our treasures – the spiritual results of our good deeds carried out on earth – are stored. "Do not store up for yourselves treasures on earth," Jesus warned, "where moths and vermin destroy, and where thieves break in and steal. But store up for yourselves treasures in heaven, where moths and vermin do not destroy, and where thieves do not break in and steal. For where your treasure is, there your heart will be also'" (Matthew 6:19-21).

In heaven God has prepared a room for us. During Jesus' discourse the evening of His arrest, He told His disciples, "'My Father's house has many rooms; if that were not so, would I have told you that I am going there to prepare a place for you?'" (John 14:2). And with our limited human understanding, we can't even imagine the magnificence, the love, and the sheer joy of what God has prepared for us: "'What no eye has seen, / what no ear has heard, / and what no human mind has conceived' – / the things God has prepared for those who love him – " (1 Corinthians 2:9).

Because heaven is God's throne room, His dwelling place, it is the source of supernatural knowledge and of all provision, like manna for the Hebrews, like salvation for His people. It is a source of hope, it is a source of wisdom. When we pray, "your kingdom come, / your will be done, / on earth as it is in heaven" (Matthew 6:10), we're imploring God to align our earthly desire with His heavenly will, to release heaven's perfection and heaven's power on a fallen earth.

"Repent: for the kingdom of heaven is at hand," Jesus preached after His baptism (Matthew 4:17 KJV). The kingdom of heaven is like a mustard seed, yeast kneaded into dough, treasure buried in a field, a merchant searching for pearls, a net cast into the sea, the owner of a house bringing out new treasures in addition to the old, a king settling accounts, a landowner hiring workers for his vineyard, a king preparing a banquet, ten virgins waiting for the bridegroom. Repent – change your way of thinking – for the kingdom of heaven is Jesus Himself! And where the King is, there is great joy, permanent and everlasting.

If joy is the presence of God, then heaven is the essence of joy: the joy of seeing the face of

God, of being surrounded by the glory of God, of falling on our face in worship of God with the multitude of saints and the heavenly host of angels. Heaven is the joy of eternal life, of everlasting relationship, of living out God's eternal and perfect will. Heaven is the culmination and continuation of our life's work, the attainment of what is hoped for, the pinnacle of our faith.

> *"'Never again will they hunger;*
> *never again will they thirst.*
> *The sun will not beat down on them,'*
> *nor any scorching heat.*
> *For the Lamb at the center of the throne*
> *will be their shepherd;*
> *'he will lead them to springs of living water.'*
> *'And God will wipe away every tear from*
> *their eyes.'"*
>
> – Revelation 7:16-17

Repent, for the kingdom of God is at hand! May the shadow of heaven cover your heart, open your eyes, and reveal itself in its holy magnificence and everlasting joy! May Paradise, for you, be found! Choose joy!

CHAPTER 21

JESUS, OUR ULTIMATE JOY

Laugh, and the world laughs with you;
Weep, and you weep alone.
— Ella Wheeler Wilcox,
"Solitude"[54]

Nehemiah said, "Go and enjoy choice food and
sweet drinks, and send some to those who have
nothing prepared. This day is holy to our Lord.
Do not grieve, for the joy of the LORD is your
strength."
— Nehemiah 8:10

Until about five years ago my experience of
Jesus, the Second Person of the Trinity, was
fuzzy at best, and downright heretical at worst. I
had no problem with God the Father, and I
wholeheartedly embraced God the Holy Spirit. I
prayed, I had faith, and even in the darkest

shadows of depression, when I dared to declare to God I didn't believe in Him anymore, I went right on believing nonetheless. But I still didn't know how to handle Jesus.

Who was this mysterious guy Who walked amongst the Hebrews more than two-thousand years ago, a man the Bible claims performed miracles, preached forgiveness of sins, and declared Himself the Son of God? Who was this person Who willingly offered His back to Roman torturers, carried the sin of mankind on His back, and allowed the Father to turn His back on Him while suffering such an inhumane death? I thought I didn't know.

But in my heart I *did* know. I think the first time I realized Jesus is Who He says He is occurred when I was in my late teens or early twenties and struggling with the scourge of worry. At that time worry had already put me in the hospital twice with bleeding ulcers, one that punched into an artery and almost killed me, requiring emergency workers to squeeze six units of blood into my right arm while in the ER. I passed out two times during that drama, and hospital staff told me more than once I was lucky to still be alive.

Quite alive, but still fighting mightily with worry, I later tried to get a handle on how to control it before it dug another hole straight through my stomach lining and pushed me into an early grave. So I began to read books on breaking the worry habit. One of those books claimed Jesus wasn't God, but merely a man who had learned how to control the power of the subconscious mind. When I read that sentence my face flushed. Anger welled up from deep within my body and my spirit. I cried "No!" and slammed the book shut. I never read another word in it, and I eventually ridded myself of it.

Unsettled, I continued to go to church, bouncing around from denomination to denomination, searching for a place I felt my heart belonged. I still embraced the Father, I still believed in the Holy Spirit, and I still tiptoed around Jesus. I was a mess. Then one day I joined an after-church discussion group to dive deeper into my religious education. In preparation for these talks, the subject eventually came around to the Person of Jesus Christ. Within a few months the discussions began to slide down the slippery path of questioning Jesus' divinity, and as the talks approached the crumbling ledge of heresy, God did a most extraordinary thing: He led me to my wife. We started dating, and after a few months we both stepped into the world of non-denominational evangelical Christian fellowship – and into the arms of Christ!

"But what about you?" [Jesus] asked.
"Who do you say I am?"
Simon Peter answered, "You are the Messiah, the Son of the living God."
Jesus replied, "Blessed are you, Simon son of Jonah, for this was not revealed to you by flesh and blood, but by my Father in heaven.
– Matthew 16:15-17

Jesus is God. Period. How many times have you heard someone describe Jesus as a "good man," that He was a prophet, that He was an influential teacher, then turn around and deny His divinity in the very next breath? "But He never came right out and said He was God!" they argue. "What Bible are you reading?" I retort. Just because He didn't say, "Hey, look at Me, I'm God," doesn't diminish the fact that He was, and still is, God! That isn't His style.

When Caiaphas, the high priest, asked Jesus point-blank, "Tell us if you are the Messiah, the Son of God," Jesus responded, "You have said so," turning it back on Caiaphas and his own capability to receive and accept the truth (Matthew 26:63b,64a). The fact that the high priest tore his robe and accused Jesus of blasphemy shows he took Jesus' response as affirmative. Don't ask the question if you can't stand the answer.

Jesus indeed made it very clear throughout Scripture, in both the Old and New Testaments, Who He truly is: "For to us a child is born, / to us a son is given, / and the government will be on his shoulders. / And he will be called Wonderful Counselor, Mighty God, / Everlasting Father, Prince of Peace" (Isaiah 9:6). "'Very truly I tell you,' Jesus answered, 'before Abraham was born, I am!'" (John 8:58). "I and the Father are one" (John 10:30). "Jesus answered, 'I am the way and the truth and the life. No one comes to the Father except through me'" (John 14:6).

"Who do you say I am?" Jesus asked the Disciples. Who do you say He is? Believing Jesus is the Son of God, our Savior and Redeemer, is a choice. God, by His mighty grace, gave us free will when He created us, the ultimate gift of a Father Who loves us more than we can ever know. And He set before us the choice: to believe or to not believe. It's up to us to decide, up to us to confess, up to us to declare. And this declaration can only come through faith.

Jesus has existed since the beginning of time, and through Him all things were made (John 1:1-3). Jesus is the Word incarnate (John 1:14), God's promise of redemption (Isaiah 53:5) Who now sits at the right hand of the Father (Hebrews 1:3, 1 Peter 3:22) and dwells in our hearts as the Spirit of God (2 Corinthians 6:16). He emptied Himself out, lowering Himself to our level, becoming a slave (Philippians 2:7) so that He could offer Himself up as the Lamb of God (John 1:29), the last atoning sacrifice (Romans 3:25, Hebrews 2:17), our High Priest dying to sin once for all (Hebrews 5:10, Hebrews 7:27). By His obedience He tore away the veil between mankind and the Creator (Matthew 27:51, Mark 15:38) and restored our relationship with Him. Jesus *is* joy.

Have you ever seen the art print called "Jesus Laughing?" I think the first time I saw that colored charcoal rendering of Jesus by Ralph Kozak, I had to look again. Jesus... *laughing*? Here was a portrayal of Jesus with His face lifted up, His eyes closed, His mouth opened so wide I could see His teeth! *Now that's what Jesus looked like,* I thought. *They finally got it right!* It was as if Mr. Kozak had captured Jesus' expression the exact moment Peter delivered the punch line of a not-so pious joke: "So he says – get this – 'Two humps are better than one.' Ha ha ha!"

In all my life I'd never seen a picture of Jesus even smiling, let alone laughing. How crazy is it that the One Who declared in John 10:10, "I have come that they may have life, and have it to the full" would be portrayed as gloomy, sullen, serious, and low-spirited in so many depictions?

The picture of God painted into my childhood experience was not that of a witty, loving, forgiving, creative, exciting Abba, but that of a stoic judge, ready to condemn me to the fires of hell for calling my brother a name or for making a funny face (yep, I got the "God's gonna freeze it like that" warning a lot during my childhood. Sorry, Mom, just saying). The images of Jesus I carried in my head were either from the life-sized 3D crucifix of a bleeding Savior hanging ominously over the church altar, ready to pounce on me for having that impure thought about the girl in the second pew on the left, or from paintings like the ones the Old Masters created, masterpieces portraying an effeminate Jesus with milky white skin, blue eyes, and long flowing brown hair, just like any self-respecting first-century Hebrew carpenter would have looked like. In all of them, Jesus never smiled. His mouth was always set in a hard line, a compassionate pucker, the grimace of pain, or the lifelessness of a horrible death. The best He could conjure north of a straight line was a smirk, like in Paolo Veronese's "The Wedding at Cana."

I think that's why "Laughing Jesus" made such an impression on me: How could the Jesus portrayed by my early experience of the Church, by the Old Masters, by hellfire and damnation, and by barely-comprehensible and never well-explained readings of the Gospel align with Ralph Kozak's vision of Jesus' personality? Could I dare believe Jesus could have been... gulp... funny? Could I dare think Jesus had an amazing sense of humor? Could I dare believe Jesus did, indeed, laugh? Of course! "Joy is Jesus to me," said Marc Owings. "They're one in the same." Yes, joy is Jesus, and Jesus is joy! And as the manifestation of joy, He has an amazing sense of humor. He has to! Just look at us! We are Genesis 1:26 conceptions, created in God's own image, including God's sense of humor in all its fullness and subtlety. We laugh because God laughed first.

Imagine this: you've been invited to a party by someone you recently met, and you don't know anyone there besides the host. You arrive a bit late to ensure your entrance will be somewhat low-key, maybe even clandestine, just in case your discomfort doesn't settle and you want to make a quick exit. You drift over to the food table and snag a paper plate full of Fritos and bean dip. You grab a glass of sweet tea, then look around for your host's familiar face. Not finding her right away, you notice three or four people standing in the dining room, lugubriosity covering their faces, nodding seriously. From the snippets of conversation you can make out, it appears to be a complaint-fest in full swing, a full-blown anti-Philippians 2:14 session. Soon you leave the room to find something more comfortable and interesting to listen to.

As you pass from the kitchen to the living area, your attention is immediately drawn to a large group of laughing people in the middle of the room, an arc of joy centered on a man standing at the focus. You linger behind the group, but through the wall of bodies you get a glimpse of him. He's swarthy, kind of short with a muscular build, black curly hair, a dark, weathered, kind and intelligent face, wearing a full beard that's oh so *Duck Dynasty*. But nestled in that curly black beard is an amazing smile, ear-to-ear. You catch his eyes, shiny dark hazel flecked with hints of gold, and you suddenly have a clear definition of what the phrase "sparkling eyes" really means.

You are instantly attracted to this person you know nothing about, but deep down you understand he's someone special just by the joy he exudes, by his relaxed and confident demeanor, and by the way he holds his Solo cup and the crowd's attention. And by the way he cuts up! What a hoot! He's got a deep laugh, full, genuine, infectious. You start to laugh with him, even though you arrived in the middle of the story he's telling and have no idea where it started at or where it's going, something about a bunch of fishermen caught in a storm on a lake. By the end of the anecdote you discover he's not only made you laugh, and laugh hard, but he's left you with a deep feeling of peace, satisfaction, and... happiness. Later that evening you finally get to visit with the host, where you realize your discomfort is completely gone and you're having fun despite your initial reservations.

That's how I picture Jesus, filled from His dusty sandaled feet to His greasy black hair with joy. He exuded it. He spoke it. He lived it. He laughed it. And why not? How could He have been such a draw if He was a stick in the mud? Even Isaiah prophesied the Messiah wouldn't be particularly attractive physically (see Isaiah 53:2), so how did he draw people in? A stick in the mud couldn't rile up hornets and prod people to open their eyes and ears to the truth if it stayed stuck in the dirt. Jesus partied. He hung out with sinners to the point the religious self-righteous accused Him of being a glutton and a drunk (see Matthew 11:10 and Luke 7:34). He had an attractive passion, a dangerous compassion. He drew crowds to himself not only because of His teaching and his miracles, but because of His personality and His laughter. God definitely has a sense of humor, and Jesus manifested it as a walking, talking picture of the Father's irony and deep love for us. Jesus wasn't what people expected, but He was exactly what we needed.

When I attended the Fully Alive event with Marc Owings in January 2011, the participants experienced not only God's redemptive power, but also His sense of humor first-hand. One of the guys, while fasting and meditating outdoors at the edge of Lake Fork, grew thirsty. "Lord" he prayed, "I sure could use a Dr Pepper right now." His eyes were suddenly drawn to the calm lake surface, where an empty Dr Pepper bottle floated up to him on the ripples.

Another asked, "Lord, I sure am cold. It would be nice to have a fire in front of me." Immediately he looked up and saw smoke drifting into the sky from a brush fire directly in front of him – a mile away on the other side of the lake!

Remember Matthew 19:13-14 (and similarly Mark 10:13-15), where Jesus rebuked the disciples for keeping the little children from coming to Him?

> *Then people brought little children to Jesus for him to place his hands on them and pray for them. But the disciples rebuked them.*
> *Jesus said, "Let the little children come to me, and do not hinder them, for the kingdom of heaven belongs to such as these."*
> – Matthew 19:13-14

This passage is generally interpreted to mean that unless we develop a complete and unquestioning (i.e., childlike) trust in God, we can't enter His Kingdom. I believe this also includes rediscovering the uninhibited joy and all-encompassing fun that comes from this freeing trust as children of God. If we can laugh at life like little children can, if we blow snot bubbles into Satan's face, we've got both feet in the Kingdom even if we sometimes feel like we're only doing the cosmic Hokey Pokey.

The New American Bible, Revised Edition translates Nehemiah 8:10 slightly different than the New International Version:

> *He continued: "Go, eat rich foods and drink sweet drinks, and allot portions to those who had nothing prepared; for today is holy to our LORD. Do not be saddened this day, for rejoicing in the LORD is your strength!"*
> – Nehemiah 8:10 (NABRE)

Rejoice in the Lord because rejoicing (expressing joy), experiencing, and living life in and for the Lord is, indeed, our strength. It's the very core of life and joy! "Rejoice in the Lord always!" the Apostle Paul commanded in Philippians 4:4. "I will say it again: Rejoice!" Why? Because He came to give us life, and to give it to us to the full.

If Jesus can laugh at the world in all its hurt, tragedy, affliction, and sickness, in all its joys, hope, love, and miracles, why shouldn't we? After all, He has already overcome the world. As my friend Gilbert Banda said, "Joy is what roots us deep in what Jesus stands for." So go use your life to paint an amazing picture for the world, and make sure you're laughing.

CHAPTER 22

SHARING OUR JOY WITH OTHERS

This little light of mine, I'm gonna let it shine.
This little light of mine, I'm gonna let it shine.
This little light of mine, I'm gonna let it shine.
Shine, shine, shine, shine, shine.
— "This Little Light of Mine,"
Harry Dixon Loes[55]

In late 2013, when Hannah was still five years old, she began to express interest in being baptized. At first I was hesitant. "She's too young," I told Mary. "I don't think she's old enough to understand what it really means to accept Jesus into your heart and be baptized." Not long after Hannah started talking to us about baptism, Pastor Scott Crenshaw announced an upcoming event at New River Fellowship, "The Big Splash," a community get-together held in the church parking lot where dozens of people would be baptized in three large inflatable pools.

"If your child is asking you to be baptized," Scott said, "don't stand in their way. As Jesus said, 'Let the little children come to me, and do not hinder them, for the kingdom of God belongs to such as these.'" Yes! If anyone can demonstrate the true meaning of what it means to express pure joy and to love and to trust God unconditionally, it's the children; they can remind us world-weary adults what it means to live out the gospel moment-by-moment.

With my reservations pulverized, we immediately signed Hannah up for the kids' baptism class, and believe me, there's nothing more refreshing than attending a lesson geared for children on the basics of what it means to be a Christ follower, a message sometimes burdened by legalism, crusted over by the realities of everyday existence, or worn out by apathy, cynicism, and laziness.

Kim Brewer, administrator and teacher in the kids' ministries at New River, presented to the young baptismal candidates a short chart pitch on the basics of sin, salvation, and baptism. To help explain the concepts, she employed the acronym KLOSS: Know Him, Love Him, Obey Him, Serve Him, and Share Him; the gospels in a nutshell. She urged the kids to worship God, attend church, learn about Him, spend time with Him, and pray. Kim taught the little ones to honor God through words and actions, and to employ the Golden Rule: "So in everything, do to others what you would have them do to you"

(Matthew 7:12a). She explained that by obeying Jesus' commands, we demonstrate our love for Him. "If you love me," Jesus said, "keep my commands" (John 14:15). She told the kids that by sharing our testimonies and our salvation stories, we live out Jesus' command to "go and make disciples of all nations" (Matthew 28:19a). And finally, she instructed the children to serve both inside and outside the church. "I have set you an example that you should do as I have done for you," Jesus told the disciples after He had washed their feet. "Very truly I tell you, no servant is greater than his master, nor is a messenger greater than the one who sent him. Now that you know these things, you will be blessed if you do them" (John 13:15-17).

After Kim finished teaching, she asked the kids several questions on the material to ensure they understood the doctrine. Hannah answered the questions, expressed a comprehension of sin and salvation, acknowledged Jesus as her Savior and Lord, and looked forward to being dunked at The Big Splash. She was excited and more than ready! So on Sunday, September 8, 2013, Josh McCasland, New River's Youth Pastor, baptized Hannah in the name of the Father, and of the Son, and of the Holy Spirit. As Pastor Josh held her nose, dipped her under the surface, and lifted her back up, Hannah was transformed, and her light has only intensified since she has become a true daughter of the Most High God and an amazing joy to everyone she touches.

From the time she was itty-bitty, Hannah has demonstrated time and again her connection to heaven, a connection that hasn't diminished as she's gotten older, but has only grown more brilliant. One early summer, before Hannah was baptized, we attended a wedding at a Catholic Cathedral. During the rehearsal at the church, Hannah grabbed the hand of one of the little girls and led her around the perimeter, pointing at the Stations of the Cross and the stained glass windows. "That's God," she explained. "That's Jesus." During those fifteen minutes Hannah became a heavenly tour guide, pointing out the Truth and providing the direction as only a wise five-year-old could do. To say Mary and I were proud of her would be an understatement; her confident witnessing spoke volumes to the wisdom of Jesus' words, "for the kingdom of God belongs to such as these."

Fast forward ten months. While at her grandma's house, the same little girl to whom Hannah had given the heavenly tour noticed flags and bells hanging from her grandma's ceiling. "What are those?" she asked, pointing.

"Those are Tibetan prayer bells and prayer flags," she explained. "They remind me to pray."

"Pray for what?" the girl queried. "Who do you pray to?"

Grandma began to explain, but the granddaughter interrupted her.

"Well, Hannah says we pray to God," she declared. "Hannah says God lives in our hearts and is all around us."

Hannah's simple explanations of spiritual concepts, delivered with confident joy, had made a strong impression, one, we pray, that will last a lifetime.

As I've mentioned in an earlier chapter, each of us is called to be a light for others to glorify God and to be examples of His grace, mercy, power, love, and joy. "'You are the light of the world,'" Jesus said. "'A town built on a hill cannot be hidden. Neither do people light a lamp and put it under a bowl. Instead they put it on its stand, and it gives light to everyone in the house. In the same way, let your light shine before others, that they may see your good deeds and glorify your Father in heaven'" (Matthew 5:14-16). And what better way is there to shine that light than to live every moment, every opportunity, and every sacrifice beaming with joy? Our light can literally save others; Kim Brewer is a perfect example of the redemptive power of that light.

"I grew up in the church," she told me. "We went to church as a family, attended Sunday school classes, and tried to do right by God." But as she entered her teenage years she began to stray. "I made seriously bad choices," she said. "I was miserable and had very low self-worth. I turned to drugs and surrounded myself with lost people to make up for the hole I felt inside."

When she was seventeen she met her husband, Clint, in high school. "We walked a crooked path through our engagement and early married life," she continued. "As we got older we had our two girls, and we started making better choices, but I still felt that something was missing. My husband was a total non-believer. I prayed occasionally, read the Bible occasionally, but I felt no connection whatsoever." But she noticed that her five year old, who attended the AWANA program at the local church with a friend, was thriving. Kim felt the pull to start attending church again, and convinced her husband to go with her.

"When we walked into the church, I literally felt like Jesus was in every person's smile, handshake, and hug that I encountered. It was as if He was saying, 'Welcome Home.' I'll never forget the feeling I had on that first Sunday. I cried the entire way through worship. As the message started, I felt the tears continue to well up and pour over. The feeling is so hard to describe – it was overwhelming, to say the least."

After service, when Kim picked up her daughter, Koryn, from the nursery, she noticed a pink sticker affixed to her shirt. "It read 'I've Been Changed!'" Kim related. "Well, that was just too much for me to handle! There I was, feeling the presence of God in every moment since walking through the door, and now I read that my child had been spiritually impacted as well!"

Kim later realized the sticker on Koryn's shirt referred to her daughter's diaper status rather than her spiritual status, "but that will never take away the feeling I had that day," she said. "That was the day the hole in my heart was filled so much that it was overflowing. My husband found Christ, our relationships with the Lord and each other have grown deeper and deeper, and our children are growing up knowing the importance of a relationship with Christ and the joy it brings a person. Even in the hard times, the joy of the Lord is our strength."

We are all called to be ambassadors for Christ, bearers of the Good News, messengers delivering the gospel, a mirror reflecting His Light. All of us have been given the hope and the obligation to deliver the message of humankind's reconciliation with our Creator. "We are therefore Christ's ambassadors," the Apostle Paul wrote to the church in Corinth, "as though God were making his appeal through us. We implore you on Christ's behalf: Be reconciled to God. God made him who had no sin to be sin for us, so that in him we might become the righteousness of God" (2 Corinthians 5:20-21).

As ambassadors, we are given the full authority to represent the One Who sent us, to speak and act on His behalf, to be Jesus to the world and to the lost. "Then Jesus came to them and said, 'All authority in heaven and on earth has been given to me. Therefore go and make disciples of all nations, baptizing them in the name of the Father and of the Son and of the Holy Spirit, and teaching them to obey everything I have commanded you. And surely I am with you always, to the very end of the age" (Matthew 28:18-20).

The joy of the Lord is, truly, our strength.

Joy is living moment-by-moment in God's presence, unafraid, despite circumstances.

Joy is waking up in the morning and rejoicing in the gift of another breath, another opportunity, another chance to serve the Kingdom, to serve the King of kings and the Lord of lords.

Joy is diving into the streams of living water and swimming to the shore of a Mighty God who loves you more than you'll ever know or understand.

Joy is residing in the glory of the Creator of the universe and knowing you can approach Him without fear and without shame.

Joy is allowing Him to hold your hand and lead you along paths of righteousness, embraced by His will and steeped in the knowledge that in Him you are more than a conqueror – by the Blood of Christ you have been purchased, and you have already overcome.

Joy is being overcome by the sheer brilliance of His plan, His light, and His guidance.

Joy is putting aside your pride, laying down your selfishness, and trusting Him with every detail of your life, a life He predestined you to live out for His glory and your pleasure.

Joy is His Word made flesh, and His Word permeating you to the core.

Joy is Jesus.

Joy is life!

REFERENCES

[1] Frost, Robert. "The Road Not Taken." *The Poetry of Robert Frost: The Collected Poems, Complete and Unabridged*. Ed. Edward Connery Lathem. New York: Holt, Rinehart and Winston, 1979. 105.

[2] Pressman, Todd Evan, Ph.D. *Radical Joy*. New York: Kensington Publishing Corp., 1999. 18.

[3] Lewis, C.S. *Surprised by Joy, The Shape of My Early Life*. Orlando, Florida: Houghton Mifflin Harcourt Publishing Company, 1955. 15.

[4] Newberry, Tommy. *The 4:8 Principle: The Secret to a Joy-Filled Life*. Carol Stream, Illinois: Tyndale House Publishers, 2007. Kindle Edition. 94.

[5] "The Force." *Wookieepedia: The Star Wars Wiki*. n.d. 7 May 2014. http://starwars.wikia.com/wiki/The_Force.

[6] Kelly, Matthew. *A Call to Joy: Living in the Presence of God*. Beacon Publishing, 1999. 43.

[7] Newberry, Tommy. *The 4:8 Principle: The Secret to a Joy-Filled Life*. Carol Stream, Illinois: Tyndale House Publishers, 2007. Kindle Edition. 142.

[8] *Dictionary of Bible Themes*. Ed. Martin H. Manser, 2009. 5 May 2014. http://www.biblegateway.com/resources/dictionary-of-bible-themes/8361-wisdom.

[9] "P.T. Barnum Quotes." *BrainyQuote*. n.d. 12 June 2013. http://www.brainyquote.com/quotes/authors/p/p_t_barnum.html.

[10] "Yir'ah." *BibleStudyTools.com*. 2014. Bible Study Tools. 17 June 2014. http://www.biblestudytools.com/lexicons/hebrew/nas/yirah.html

[11] "Phobeo." *BibleStudyTools.com*. 2014. Bible Study Tools. 17 June 2014. http://www.biblestudytools.com/lexicons/greek/kjv/phobeo.html

[12] "Phobos." *BibleStudyTools.com*. 2014. Bible Study Tools. 17 June 2014. http://www.biblestudytools.com/lexicons/greek/kjv/phobos.html

[13] Aquinas, St. Thomas. *The Summa Theologica of St. Thomas Aquinas.* 2nd and Revised Editions. Trans. Fathers of the English Dominican Province. 1920. Chapter 19: "The Gift of Fear," Article 2. Online Edition 2008, Kevin Knight. 5 May 2014. http://www.newadvent.org/summa/3019.htm.

[14] Houdmann, S. Michael. "What is true worship?" *GotQuestions.org*. n.d. 23 December 2013. http://www.gotquestions.org/true-worship.html#ixzz2oJ1I1kO3.

[15] Driscoll, Mark. "What is Worship?" *Resurgence*. 23 January 2011. Mars Hill Church. 30 December 2013. http://theresurgence.com/2011/01/23/what-is-worship.

[16] Kelly, Matthew. *A Call to Joy: Living in the Presence of God*. Beacon Publishing, 1999. 122.

[17] "Stories of Transformation." *New River*. n.d. New River Fellowship. 2 January 2014. http://newriver.tv/media/stories//page2/. Used with permission of Jason Hoffman and New River Fellowship (www.newriver.tv).

[18] Ibid.

[19] Ibid.

[20] Ibid.

[21] Ibid.

[22] "Quotable Quote." *goodreads.com*. 2014. Good Reads Inc. 17 June 2014. https://www.goodreads.com/quotes/236822-the-glory-of-god-is-a-human-being-fully-alive.

[23] Kelly, Matthew. *A Call to Joy: Living in the Presence of God*. Beacon Publishing, 1999. 124.

[24] Peale, Norman Vincent. *The Power of Positive Thinking*. New York: Ballantine Books, 1982. 20.

[25] Ibid.

[26] Ibid. 22.

[27] Young, Sarah. *Jesus Calling: Enjoying Peace in His Presence*. Nashville: Thomas Nelson, 2004. 341.

[28] Eldredge, John. *Beautiful Outlaw: Experiencing the Playful, Disruptive, Extravagant Personality of Jesus*. New York: FaithWords, 2011. 51.

[29] Oliver, Myrna and Valerie J. Nelson. "Art Linkletter dies at 97; broadcasting pioneer created 'Kids Say the Darndest Things.'" *Los Angeles Times*. 27 May 2010. 9 May 2014. http://www.latimes.com/local/obituaries/la-me-art-linkletter-new-20100527-story.html#page=1.

[30] "Johann Wolfgang von Goethe > Quotes > Quotable Quote." *goodreads.com*. 2014. Good Reads Inc. 17 June 2014. https://www.goodreads.com/quotes/929-whatever-you-can-do-or-dream-you-can-begin-it.

[31] "George Santayana." *Wikiquote*. 9 June 2014. 17 June 2014. http://en.wikiquote.org/wiki/George_Santayana.

[32] Toews, Rockford E. "One Less Accountant." *The Thoreau Reader*. 2001. 12 February 2014. http://thoreau.eserver.org/oneless.html.

[33] Kelly, Matthew. *A Call to Joy: Living in the Presence of God*. Beacon Publishing, 1999. 77.

[34] Khurana, Simran. "'Star Wars' Quotes: The Magic of 'Star Wars:' Quotes Recreate the Magic." *About.com Quotations*. n.d. 9 May 2014. http://quotations.about.com/od/moviequotes/a/starwars1.htm.

[35] Kelly, Matthew. *A Call to Joy: Living in the Presence of God*. Beacon Publishing, 1999. 117.

[36] Strong, James. *The New Strong's Complete Dictionary of Bible Words*. Nashville, Tennessee: Thomas Nelson Publishers, 1996. 635.

[37] Kelly, Matthew. *A Call to Joy: Living in the Presence of God*. Beacon Publishing, 1999. 154.

[38] "Bill Cosby: Himself (1983) Quotes." *IMDb*. n.d. 11 June 2014. http://www.imdb.com/title/tt0083652/quotes.

[39] Barnett, Caroline. *Willing to Walk on Water*. Carol Stream, Illinois: Tyndale House Publishers, 2013. 218.

[40] Kelly, Matthew. *A Call to Joy: Living in the Presence of God*. Beacon Publishing, 1999. 134.

[41] "Mother Teresa Quotes." *BrainyQuote*. n.d. 12 June 2014. http://www.brainyquote.com/quotes/authors/m/mother_teresa.html.

[42] "Greta Garbo > Quotes > Quotable Quote." *goodreads.com*. 2014. Good Reads Inc. 19 June 2014. https://www.goodreads.com/quotes/252365-anyone-who-has-a-continuous-smile-on-his-face-conceals

References

43 Young, Sarah. *Jesus Calling: Enjoying Peace in His Presence*. Nashville: Thomas Nelson, 2004. 301.

44 "The Apostle James (Son of Zebedee)." *BiblePath.com*. n.d. 6 November 2013. www.biblepath.com/james.html.

45 Spurgeon, C.H. "The Oil of Joy for Mourning," Sermon #3341. *Spurgeon Gems & Other Treasures of God's Truth*. 13 February 1913. Metropolitan Tabernacle Pulpit. 19 June 2014. http://www.spurgeongems.org/vols58-60/chs3341.pdf.

46 "Martin Luther > Quotes > Quotable Quote." *goodreads.com*. 2014. Good Reads Inc. 19 June 2014. https://www.goodreads.com/quotes/215399-god-writes-the-gospel-not-in-the-bible-alone-but.

47 "Eleonora Duse." *Wikipedia: The Free Encyclopedia*. 18 May 2014. 12 June 2014. http://en.wikipedia.org/wiki/Eleonora_Duse.

48 "Regarded Quotes." *BrainyQuote*. n.d. 7 May 2014. http://www.brainyquote.com/quotes/keywords/regarded.html.

49 Browne, Thomas, Sir. *Religio Medici*. Vol. III, Part 5. The Harvard Classics. New York: P.F. Collier & Son, 1909–14; Bartleby.com, 2001. 12 June 2014. www.bartleby.com/3/5/.

50 Thoreau, Henry David. *Walden*. Public Domain, 2012. 66. Kindle Edition.

51 Kelly, Matthew. *A Call to Joy: Living in the Presence of God*. Beacon Publishing, 1999. 120.

52 "Searchable Paradise Lost." *Paradise Lost Study Guide*. 1999. New Arts Library. 12 June 2014. http://www.paradiselost.org.

53 "Heaven Quotes: quotations about Heaven." *NotableQuotes*. n.d. 4 April 2014. http://www.notable-quotes.com/h/heaven_quotes.html.

[54] "POEM: Solitude by Ella Wheeler Wilcox."
PoemHunter.com. 3 January 2003. 12 June 2014.
http://www.poemhunter.com/poem/solitude/.

[55] "This Little Light of Mine." *Wikipedia: The Free
Encyclopedia.* 24 May 2014. 12 June 2014.
http://en.wikipedia.org/wiki/This_Little_Light_of_Mine.

ABOUT THE AUTHOR

David C. Hughes defies the premise that engi-
neers can't write. With over three decades of
writing experience and more than 25 years of
technical writing and editing experience, David
left his full-time corporate job in 2013 to launch
his writing career. He has a passion for writing
and for other writers, and loves to "talk shop"
with anyone who will listen.

A former youth leader and deacon, David's life is resolutely defined by his pursuit of God, and his desire is to convey God's love, joy, grace, and healing through his testimony. His blog site, "David C. Hughes, Writer," broadcasts his latest take on what it means to be a Christ-centered man, husband, father, son, brother, and friend in these exciting and challenging times.

Originally from the town of Maine, New York, David now lives near Aledo, Texas with the loves of his life: his wife, Mary, and his daughter, Hannah. At last count he also has two dogs, a handful of fish, five chickens, two guinea pigs, and countless fire ants.

To check out David's latest projects, thoughts, and musings, please visit his blog at http://davidchugheswriter.com.